TEACHINGS OF
PEYOTE
SHAMANS

TEACHINGS OF THE
PEYOTE SHAMANS

The Five Points of Attention

JAMES ENDREDY

Park Street Press
Rochester, Vermont • Toronto, Canada

Park Street Press
One Park Street
Rochester, Vermont 05767
www.ParkStPress.com

Park Street Press is a division of Inner Traditions International

Library of Congress Cataloging-in-Publication Data
Endredy, James.
   Teachings of the peyote shamans : the five points of attention / James Endredy.
     pages cm
    Summary: "A rare in-depth look at the inner workings of Huichol shamanism"
—Provided by publisher.
   ISBN 978-1-62055-461-6 (paperback) — ISBN 978-1-62055-462-3 (e-book)
   1. Huichol Indians—Religion. 2. Huichol Indians—Rites and ceremonies. 3.
Huichol cosmology. 4. Shamanism—Mexico. 5. Peyotism—Mexico. I. Title.
   F1221.H9E64 2015
   299'.784544—dc23

                        2015014793

Printed and bound in the United States

10 9 8 7 6 5 4 3 2

Text design and layout by Priscilla Baker
This book was typeset in Garamond Premier Pro with Myriad Pro used as a display
typeface

Photo of Huichol gourd bowl on page 98 used with permission from Cheryl's
Trading Post (www.cherylstradingpost.com)

To send correspondence to the author of this book, mail a first-class letter to the
author c/o Inner Traditions • Bear & Company, One Park Street, Rochester, VT
05767, and we will forward the communication, or contact the author directly at
www.JamesEndredy.com.

Contents

 # Foreword

In the late 1980s, my wife, Lena, and I, through fortuitous circumstances, embarked on a ten-year apprenticeship with Guadalupe Candelario, an accomplished Huichol *marakáme* (singing shaman) and *kawitéro* (elected elder). His decision to teach us came from revelations and dreams given to him directly from his ancestors through ingesting the sacred peyote cactus in ceremony. So strict was our required discipline that for ten years we were not allowed to breathe a word of our visits with him to anyone including our closest friends and families. Throughout our meetings we were required by him to pretend we did not know him when other Huichol were present. We were to avoid running into groups of Huichol at all the sites deep in Mexico where the Huichol practice their traditional ceremonies. Because of this, we had to visit these sites in the desert and in the mountains in the deepest of winter in freezing, howling weather. We were required to learn in total secrecy because Huichol politics frowned on outsiders studying or learning about Huichol traditional knowledge. I have no doubt that had he not passed away from bone cancer contracted because of the toxic insecticides of the tobacco fields, our studies with him would have continued for much longer. As it is, we have continued to remain close with his extended family and have managed to deepen our relationship with the Huichol ways.

In light of our own experiences and the difficulties of learning about the Huichol way of life, the amount of personal experience and inside information James Endredy has compiled and shared in this powerful book is truly amazing. In no way has this been an easy journey for him, and you will only glimpse the sacrifices he has made to bring this compelling story to you.

Not only is his book highly informative and accurate about the Huichol way of life, but it includes profound dialogues about the Huichol's philosophy and perspective about the nature of God, the Huichol understanding of Catholicism, their beliefs about the contributions of Jesus and the Virgin Mary, and even their perceptions of comparative religions.

Here you will find rare glimpses into the details of the deer hunt and its meaning; the Huichol style of peyote ceremony and how it compares with the style of the Native American Church in the North; the five most important Huichol ceremonial sites and their relationship to the Huichol process of becoming an awakened human being; the Huichol style of governance and how their shamans perform service; and much, much more.

On a more poignant note, James Endredy carefully elucidates the endangerment of the peyote plant through overconsumption, the intrusions by outsiders onto Huichol ceremonial lands, and the pressures of the modern world that they have to face and deal with that directly threaten their way of life. He manages to cover this territory in a compelling story form so that it is never a dull recounting of facts and events but a true shamanic adventure that is hard to put down.

I have no doubt that this book will become a classic for those interested in the Huichol ways and how to understand their deep insights into nature, balance, harmony, and grand beauty.

JOSÉ LUIS STEVENS

JOSÉ LUIS STEVENS, PH.D., is the author of *Awaken the Inner Shaman, Secrets of Shamanism,* and *The Power Path.* He lectures internationally, often speaking on the subject of the indigenous wisdom of shamans and how this knowledge applies to the modern world. He is the president and cofounder of The Power Path, an international consulting firm based in Santa Fe, New Mexico.

Acknowledgments

Jacki and Sasha, thank you for making this book possible.

Jon Graham, Jeanie Levitan, and all the brilliant minds at Inner Traditions • Bear & Company, including Jessie Wimett, Kelly Bowen, Erica Robinson, Nicki Champion, Blythe Bates, and Jamaica Burns Griffin, your contributions were invaluable for the creation of this book. The spirit of the hikuri honors you.

 # Introduction

This is a book about my experiences with the peyote (pay·o·tay) shamans of western Mexico, specifically the Huichol indigenous society, and some of the core shamanic teachings I have learned from them. Although this book unfolds as a story, it's best to begin with a brief overview of who the Huichol are, in order to give geographic and historical perspectives on the following narrative.

The Huichol

The aboriginal people known as the Huichol (whee·chol′) to the outside world call themselves Wixrarika or Wixaritari (plural) in their own language. For simplicity, I will use the common name of Huichol throughout this book, although for me I consider their native culture as a whole to be Huichol and those that still live traditional lifestyles in the mountains to be Wixrarika. This distinction is complicated but may become more apparent as this book rolls along.

Unlike most aboriginal cultures in Mexico, and I daresay throughout the world, the Huichol have, for the most part, resisted missionary attempts to Christianize them. To this day, through centuries of continuous evangelical pressure, the main ceremonial centers of the Huichol retain and maintain their aboriginal, temple-ritual cycle and traditional worldview. Huichol are highly adaptable and for this reason Jesus Christ (*Jesucristo* to them) and a few other Christian figures have been included in their religious pantheon but strictly on their own terms.

The Huichol inhabit what is called the Sierra of the Nayar, or the Gran Nayar. This is a large cultural region of western Mexico that includes portions of the Mexican states of Jalisco, Nayarit, Durango, and Zacatecas. The Mexican government recognizes the "administrational" units of the Huichol to include the three major communities of San Andres Cohamiata (Tateikie), Santa Catarina Cuexcomatitlan (Tuapurie), and San Sebastian Teponahuastlan (Wauta). Added to these are the newer districts of Guadalupe Ocotan emerging from San Andres, and Tuxpan de Boloños from San Sabastian. Together these constitute the core communities of the Huichol, overseeing approximately twenty ceremonial centers. There are also more recent settlements farther away in Durango and Nayarit including Potrero, Brasiles, Puerto Guamuchil, Bancos de Calítique, Fortines, Tierra Blanca, and Zoquipan. Farthest from the Huichol homeland both physically and spiritually are those Huichol who have moved to urban areas such as Mexico City, Guadalajara, Puerto Vallarta, and the like. Current estimates place the total Huichol population between eighteen and twenty thousand. This makes them one of the smaller indigenous groups in Mexico and tiny compared to the Nahuatl and Yucatec Maya, both having populations estimated at well over two million.

Huichol live in dispersed ranches throughout the Sierra in nuclear family units. Family units are joined together by the family shrine, called a *rirriki*. These family shrines often look identical to the houses on the ranches. Communities are formed through cooperation and agreements between various families' rirrikis and joined together by the ceremonial center, called the *tuki* or *kalliway*. The Huichol I have been closely associated with throughout my life are those from the community of Santa Catarina, which has three main ceremonial centers: Tuapurie (Santa Catarina), Xawiepa (Pochotita), and Keruwitia (Las Latas). I consider

Keruwitia and Xaweipa two of the most preserved and traditional ceremonial centers of all the Huichol due to geographic location and difficulty in access; strong traditional leadership at both the level of the rirriki and kalliway; and amazing spiritual elders called kawitéros.

There are two types of governing systems in the Huichol Sierra, each very different from the other but both related to what is termed a *cargo system*. Elected people are required to carry the load (cargo) of a specific position for a specific period of time. Unlike the culture I was brought up in where officials run for office and spend countless dollars on political campaigns to get elected for mostly selfish reasons, the Huichol do not get paid for their post. It is a cargo that may in some moments carry a small amount of prestige but in general it is a burden that is considered very honorable to carry but has no financial gain. Those that put in multiple cargos in their life are highly regarded in the community simply because their service is an act of generosity combined with the desire to keep the community healthy and whole.

Elected officials that are required by the Mexican government include a governor, judge, head of security, head of agriculture, and various lesser posts including territorial mayors and sheriffs. Each post has its own special *vara* (staff) with colored ribbons signifying the various posts that are held by the officials during official meetings and events. This system was brought and imposed by the Spaniards that colonized Mexico, and now hundreds of years later, it is still enforced by the Mexican government. The government of Mexico requires the indigenous people, including the Huichol, to fill out census reports, elect officials, and acquiesce to random visits and inspections by Mexican authorities. I have experienced helicopter inspections on communities living so far off the grid in the mountains that it was truly appalling to witness, as these people have basically nothing for industrial society to exploit.

On the other hand, the Huichol have never lost their true hierarchy of decision making. At the core center of Huichol communities is a pre-Hispanic system of cargo holders led by the kawitéros. Each major temple district usually has five kawitéros who are mostly marakámes but are always older men who have the greatest knowledge of the tradition and have served many religious cargos throughout their lives. These elders are considered the embodiment of the exceptional ancestors and have the respect and obedience of the entire community. When the community designates a man a kawitéro, it is a lifelong position of the highest esteem but it also carries the most responsibilities.

Under the kawitéros are the marakámes who lead the current five-year cargo cycle. There are always at least two of these singing shaman—one that sings for the dry season ceremonies and one for the wet season. The Huichol divide their ceremonies in this way because all of their activities revolve around their agrarian lifestyle of growing corn, beans, and squash. The most important thing to any Huichol is the rain that gives life to the crops. Therefore the most important responsibility of the marakámes is to draw the rain from the cardinal directions. This is accomplished by making pilgrimages to the sacred sites of each direction and holding specific ceremonies throughout the year in the ceremonial centers.

Their sacred calendar of ceremonies and pilgrimages is so complex it would take many volumes to cover the subject adequately, and that is certainly not the aim of this book. Suffice to say that the Huichol living in the core areas of their homeland live in a separate reality from those of us living within industrial society. Practically everything they do has a spiritual context. To them, there is no division between sacred and secular. The Huichol believe that their annual cycle of ceremonies and pilgrimages serves to produce health and balance not only within their communities but also for the entire world.

Led by the elders and the marakámes are the *jicareros* (hee·ca·reh·ros). The jicareros, including the two principal marakámes, are responsible for all the yearly ceremonies and pilgrimages for a period of five years. After their five-year period is over, the kawitéros will choose the new group through their dreams and consensus. This five-year period is referred to as a cargo, in a similar way as that of the civil authorities, although being a jicarero is much more demanding and the civil positions usually run for only one year.

Each jicarero is identified by a specific ancestor deity that they embody in all the ceremonies, pilgrimages, and even in daily life for the five-year cargo period. The name *jicarero* comes from the fact that each ancestor deity has their own votive gourd bowl called a *jicara*. This jicara is passed to the new cargo holders at the end of the five-year period. The jicareros of the ceremonial centers I have been associated with number around thirty for each cycle.

Other sacred paraphernalia of the jicareros include a small gourd with hole and stopper at the top, which is used to carry a special type of ceremonial tobacco and represents the Grandfather Fire; a small circular mirror that is usually but not always worn as a necklace and that enables the jicarero to communicate directly with the ancestor deity of their jicara; and *morals* (handwoven bags with one pocket and a shoulder strap) to carry their sacred items, offerings, and other necessities on pilgrimages.

There are three basic groups or levels of jicareros. When walking to pilgrimage sites, the jicareros always take a special order. The first are the leaders of the group—the elders and marakámes and the jicareros associated with the most important ancestor deities. This is usually five to eleven men. Next are the musicians* and those singing second, or in response, to the marakámes. Then come the hunters who are associated with wolves. In the end are the youngest pilgrims, usually teenagers, but among them walks one of the leaders representing Father Sun.

The Huichol have hundreds if not thousands of sacred sites. To a Huichol every rock, tree, bird, or flower is sacred. However, there are five main sacred sites that the jicareros must visit and are the destinations of the major pilgrimages. These represent the five cardinal directions—East, West, North, South, and Center—and the corresponding ancestor deities that reside in each place. More details about this will unfold during the course of this book.

---

*Huichol play small handmade violins and guitars.

Peyote

The term peyote (*Lophophora williamsii*) traces its etymology to the Nahuatl (Aztec) word *peyutl,* but is called *hikuri* by the Huichol.* It is a small, spineless cactus with a long root. It grows in a round shape and most commonly has ribs, or sections, running from the middle to the edge. The most common type of peyote used among the Huichol also has little white tufts that appear growing in each section. The peyote cactus only appears naturally in northeastern Mexico and a small area in southwestern Texas, United States. Its range in these areas was historically much larger, but human harvesting of this slow-growing entheogen by both indigenous cultures and modern recreational users has reduced the habitat of the sacred cactus to endangered status.

The sacred peyote cactus has long been used in Mesoamerican culture. The oldest archaeological evidence of use dates back to around 5,000 BCE, although some sites may be as old as 10,500 BCE. Ethnographic reports from sixteenth- and seventeenth-century chroniclers show that the first Spanish invaders found the Aztec culture still using it in their sacred rituals thousands of years later. And it is still used today among many native peoples, most notably by the Huichol and much more recently the Native American Church and its many offshoots in the United States and Canada.

Peyote, along with other entheogens such as ayahuasca and datura, has often been called a plant of the gods. The important difference between plant entheogens and so-called normal plants are the active principles of plant entheogens that relate to hormones of the human brain. For example, mescaline, the psychoactive chemical compound found in the sacred peyote cactus, is closely related to the brain hormone norepinephrine, which belongs to the group of physiological agents known as neurotransmitters. Neurotransmitters function in the transmission of impulses between nerve cells in the brain. Interestingly,

---

*I will use both terms interchangeably.

mescaline (in the peyote cactus) and norepinephrine (in the brain) have the same chemical structure. Chemically, they are both derivatives of what chemists term phenylethylamine. The essential amino acid phenylalanine, another derivative of phenylethylamine, is widely distributed in the human body during an orgasm. In terms of shamanism and sacred usage of plant entheogens, this is far more than mere chance. Having the same basic structure as powerful hormones of the human brain, when ingested they are like keys opening the locks of doors to brain sites that alter our states of consciousness. They stimulate areas of our consciousness that usually lie dormant.

Plant entheogens such as peyote are ingested to depersonalize the experience of reality without loss of consciousness; rather, they act to help expand consciousness into multidimensional universes with infinite possibilities and realities. The most profound of these states produces deep changes in the way a person perceives reality, space, and time and how we all fit into the greater web of life surrounding us.

The Huichol marakámes use the sacred peyote cactus in all of their major ceremonies (fiestas) and at times also during the planting and sowing of their crops. Peyote serves as a major element that unifies and helps to preserve the traditional values, beliefs, and therefore, health of the tribe. In my experience with the Huichol, the peyote ceremonies that revolve around this sacred plant instill the spiritual aspects of life into all members of the community, thereby reinforcing their place in the world both as individuals and as a community. This replaces the existential void commonly found in modern society with a grounded psychological framework and worldview. It is also my opinion that the ritual use of the mind-expanding peyote has contributed to the Huichol's ability to preserve their traditions to the current day despite centuries of evangelistic pressure. The Huichol, with peyote as a central part of their spiritual tradition, are able to fluidly integrate and adapt to cultural and religious pressures that surround them.

This last point is especially important to this narrative because the teachings described in this book are not about how to use peyote.

They revolve around the disciplined use of attention, specifically the *expanded* use of attention that produces higher states of awareness and perception. The fluidness with which Huichol respond to changing circumstances stems from their expanded view of reality. Without the disciplined use of attention and the heightened awareness that comes from such practices, the use of peyote becomes meaningless.

Content

All the people and places in this book are real. The conversations, stories, and teachings are all true. I have changed the names of the main characters in the spirit of anonymity and respect for the privacy of my friends and teachers. Events have been rearranged and in a few places *slightly* altered to conform to the narrative line of the story and protect the identity of the individuals involved.

The contents of this book are in no way to be taken as a work of anthropology or ethnology, simply because I am not a scientist or academic investigator. On the contrary, where scientists and academics have gone to *investigate* the Huichol, I go to *participate*. For this reason many of the experiences, teachings, and lessons included in this book will be novel even for those familiar with the Huichol. I have been blessed with the opportunity on many occasions to participate intimately in the activities and ceremonies of these fascinating people, and it has changed me for the better.

I am nowhere even close to being fluent in the Huichol language, although I do understand a lot more than I can speak. Luckily for me, most Huichol also speak Spanish at various levels, but many of the Huichol in this book are completely fluent and that is how I communicate with them. However, as good as their Spanish or my Spanish may be, it is still a second language for both of us. I bring this up because I am aware that in certain circumstances words simply cannot be translated correctly or thoroughly. I have done my best to translate from Spanish and Huichol to English and at times have sought others to help me with difficult words and phrases. Many of the Huichol terms used in this book are contained in the glossary, which I hope will prove a helpful resource.

As I already mentioned, I am not an anthropologist so I don't walk around with a tape recorder, taking field notes. On some occasions with the Huichol, I have tried to keep a personal diary but many times it was simply impossible. Most of what I write about in this and all my other books comes from my memory. I also use a technique of recapitulation to relive experiences in a trance state.

I hope, through this book, to share with you some mind-expanding experiences that may be of value in your own life. Many concepts and techniques of indigenous cultures can be employed in the modern world to make our lives richer and more authentic.

It is also my great desire to raise awareness of the plight of the peyote cactus, which is so important for a great many people. Without protection, wise use, and changes in legislation regarding cultivation, the sacred peyote will be yet another casualty in the mass extinctions caused by humans.

Writing this, my eighth book, has been extremely enlightening and enjoyable. My wish is that it will be for you as well.

Many blessings on *your* journey,

 # The Pillory

Completely stunned by what was happening to me, I tried futilely to blow upward from my mouth in order to chase the sweat from my eyes, for I did not have the use of my hands. I was in a pillory, an ancient torture device similar to, yet more brutal than, the stocks.* With stocks one is held in place by boards that are anchored to the ground with holes for holding a seated prisoner by the legs. By contrast, the pillory is constructed with hinged wooden boards forming holes through which my head and arms were inserted, then the boards were locked together to secure me. I was completely immobilized, in the full sun of Mexico in April, sweating, and in pain.

However, as much as the pillory causes pain after many hours or days of immobility in the strained posture of being bent over with your arms trapped in front of you and your head trapped so you can't move it, the main objective of the pillory is public humiliation. And yes, I was feeling completely humiliated and totally frightened. The pillory I was forcibly put into was right on the central thoroughfare across from the main temple and in view of the ancient church, and also the government building of a Huichol community and ceremo-

---

*Both the stocks and the pillory were brought to the New World during the Spanish conquest.

nial center, in an extremely remote area of the western Sierra Madres.

For some reason there were hundreds of people gathered in this ceremonial center where only a few people actually lived. The Huichol live in small ranch communities spread across vast areas and come together in large numbers only for special events. They sometimes travel many days through the mountains to attend these events and fiestas. It occurred to me that this was certainly one of those events, although at that moment I didn't know what it was about. Although historically I knew that the pillory device was used for public humiliation, as people passing by the captured person would often throw things at them like rotten food, eggs, stones, or excrement, the Huichol passing by me simply laughed or made snide comments like "Welcome to the Sierra" or "How do you like the Sierra now, gringo?"

In my humbled state, I racked my brain trying to figure out what was going on. I tilted my head up as far as I could and in the sunlight caught a glimpse of a strange apparition that was similar to paintings and stained-glass images I had seen of the Virgin Mary. Being raised Catholic, seeing Mary in the sunlight had me quite confused because during my years of church attendance and catechism I never really experienced anything divine except for the feeling of holiness or devotion one gets when in a beautiful church or during a particularly moving mass. That's one of the reasons I researched other spiritual traditions at an early age; I had found my divine connection through nature and cultures with nature-based spirituality such as the Huichol. But I didn't have much time to think about all this as just then a stout Huichol in full ceremonial regalia followed by a group of younger men approached me. This was the first time I met Jesús.

In his ceremonial apparel—which included an intricately embroidered pants-and-shirt combo depicting sacred animals, corn, birds, peyote, and peyote-inspired designs of amazing colors; a thick woven belt of wool with complex peyote-inspired symbols; three morals woven with peyote-inspired representations of ancestor gods; and the round straw hat decorated with tufts and balls of red and blue wool typically worn by shamans and ceremonial leaders—and also by his demeanor, it was apparent to me that he was a man of importance and most likely a marakáme, a Huichol shaman, healer, and holy man. He addressed me and I was informed that I had broken their traditional laws and had to stand before the Governmental Council and explain myself. I was released from the pillory and given some water to drink in the shade. Slowly I began to recall how I had gotten into this position.

It was early April and I was sitting with some Huichol friends in the small Mexican town of Huejuquilla El Alto, which was the town nearest to where my Huichol friends live in the mountains. Some Huichol had come down from the mountains to buy yarn and other materials for their artwork while the others waited for them in the main plaza. They were from a ceremonial center and ranchos in a part of the Sierra I didn't know very well, but I had met them many times in my travels and in the towns of Huejuquilla and Mezquitic in the state of Jalisco. They enjoyed speaking to me, a *gringo tewari* (non-Huichol, non-Mexican white guy) familiar to some extent with Huichol culture, to hear about the goings-on in the outside world.

With their purchases complete, they said adios and began their trip back to their ranchos. I wandered around the market for a while and then sat at an outdoor table of one of the few restaurants in town. A few minutes later, an elderly woman with a distinctly German accent approached me and in English said, "Excuse me, but I was watching earlier when you were speaking to the Natives and I'm wondering if I could ask you a few questions regarding them?"

I halfheartedly agreed to her request (Huichol are notorious for their privacy and one way to surely lose their trust is to speak about them behind their backs) and invited her to join me. Ines was a short but large-boned woman with a flair for the dramatic. Her English was terrific but she knew almost no Spanish, and I wondered how she had made it this far into the Sierra without knowing the language. But I soon found out she had lots of money, and money can get you many places where language alone cannot.

She went on to explain in a flamboyant manner that she was totally intrigued with the Huichol: their way of life, their artwork, their clothing, and their religion. Ines wanted to help them in some way but didn't know how. She had first encountered the Huichol culture when a museum in Germany held an exhibit of Huichol artwork and the artist, Rosendo, was there as well.

Coincidently this particular Rosendo was a friend of mine, and I had invited him to my house in Pennsylvania for a few weeks many years before but had not seen him recently. For a Huichol, Rosendo was considered materially rich. He owned a pickup truck, had cattle and goats, and often traveled abroad to sell his artwork. But I also knew Rosendo in the traditional way. His father was a famous marakáme and he himself had been a jicarero twice (totaling ten years of service to the temple) and also held one-year government cargos when appointed to him. Ines didn't directly ask me to take her to Rosendo, she didn't even know that I knew him and I didn't tell her, but I could tell that's where this discussion was heading. I casually explained to her about how private the Huichol are and that it can take many years of acquaintance before they accept that you aren't simply trying to get something from them or photograph them.

"But I'm here to do just the opposite," she replied. "I have been blessed financially, I'm getting on in years, and I want to share my good fortune in ways that will actually help the things I appreciate in this life. I believe that helping to preserve the Huichol culture is one of those things."

I had been down this road before, both in my own desire to help my Huichol friends in preserving their homeland and sacred sites and also with trying to help others that wanted to help them. It's a tricky and very political process that many people, including me, have found to be frustrating and confusing. Long before meeting Ines, I decided that the best way for me to be of support to Huichol culture was to simply help out those Huichol who were continuing the ancient traditions and who were my friends. In other words, I did not attempt to help the whole Huichol nation because that is a job better done by NGOs and government programs, but instead to support specific projects that included my intimate friends and mentors.

Ines was very astute and could feel my reluctance. She offered to pay me for my services. "I need a guide while here in the Sierra and I don't take auspicious encounters with people that happen at the perfect time lightly," Ines said in a very formal tone. "I believe we were meant to meet here at this moment. I'm hoping you will help me in this endeavor and I can pay you for your time," she added.

"That's a very kind gesture," I replied, "But I have only two days left here and then I'm going back to Mexico City where I have some business to attend to."

"Well, when will you be here again? I had hoped to rent an apartment here and stay a few months."

"I could come back in a couple weeks but I wasn't planning to," I replied.

"Please come back! I'll make you a deal. I'll pay for your travel expenses to and from Mexico City, and in return, just help me find a suitable place to stay here while you're gone. This way, I can learn about the culture here and also hire a Spanish teacher and try and learn some of the language."

Ines's enthusiasm was contagious, and I had not a doubt in my mind that she would stay her course and do what she said even though this was one of the most rural parts of Mexico. I too was of the same opinion regarding chance meetings that seemingly happened at the perfect time. At that time, the extra money Ines was willing to offer would be put to good use and extend my stay in Mexico. So, with some trepidation I agreed to her request, and after a few days of inquiries, I found a suitable location for her to live. Actually for this part of the country it was quite fabulous, a place I would love to have, but hardly fancy by modern standards. It was basically a small, second-floor flat in a nice house, with a sufficient bathroom and equipped with a propane stove for cooking and sparsely furnished with rustic furniture.

But the main reason I rented it for Ines was that I felt it was a safe place. The town of Huejuquilla has many upstanding residents, but unfortunately a wealthy foreign woman in this part of Mexico was not safe from many people who would think nothing of taking advantage of her for her money—or even doing her physical harm. Plus, Ines didn't know this, but Rosendo, the same Rosendo she previously spoke of and who was my good friend, rented the apartment below hers for use when he was in town. He was almost never there, but I spoke with his sons and relatives who mostly used the place and they promised to keep an eye on Ines for me. After looking for days, I was totally satisfied with this arrangement. Rosendo's family knew everyone around and would not let anything happen to Ines in my absence. Of course I paid them for their service.

I went to Mexico City and returned to the Sierras a couple of weeks later. I found Ines in the plaza and, after speaking with her, it was clear that she had made some friends and had learned some Spanish. She was more excited than ever to go into the mountains with me as her guide. To my surprise, when I arrived in Huejuquilla I saw none of my Huichol friends.

Her desire to visit the Huichol on their home turf was fervent and I finally succumbed. In considering the most appropriate manner to do so, I thought of my first Huichol friend. I first met Tayau (the name he was given as jicarero of the Sun) when studying with Victor Sanchez in the mountains outside Mexico City. Little known to me at the time, my new friend was a high-ranking official. He was the current president of the Union of Jicareros of Jalisco.

Tayau, whom I have written about in previous books, was a young man in his late twenties but held one of the most important offices in all of the Huichol territory. Whenever Tayau offered me a chance to visit his homeland, no Huichol ever bothered me about what I was doing there. I went on my first two pilgrimages to the peyote fields of Wirikuta with Tayau. The Huichol Tayau—the elected representative of the jicareros over a vast region including the three largest Huichol communities—and the gringo tewari James, explorer and wisdom seeker, had a connection beyond words or reason. He knew as well as I that our friendship was put together by forces we couldn't imagine.

Due to her genuine desire and the knowledge that her intent was to donate money for legitimate Huichol programs or ceremonies, I guess I overlooked, or thought I could overlook, the strict protocol for entering the Huichol Sierra with a stranger in tow. With glaring looks from the Huichol, we boarded the beaten-up Huichol school bus that carried people from the mountains into town and back again, usually once a day. My plan was to go to the main ceremonial center of Santa Catarina by way of Nueva Colonia and the ceremonial center of Las Latas.

The two-hour bus ride from Huejuquilla on barely passable dirt roads would drop us off in Nueva Colonia. This was a Huichol community with access to the outside world. Nueva Colonia has one of the grade schools in the Sierra run by the Mexican government and also a government-run health clinic. For me it was the starting point for reaching the ceremonial centers hidden in the mountains. From Nueva Colonia we would walk most of a day through the mountains to the ceremonial center of Las Latas, where I had good friends. Once there, we might be able to find information about the whereabouts of Tayau, who spent most of his time traveling throughout the vast Sierra and was often hard to find on short notice. In any case, from Las Latas we could walk to Santa Catarina, the seat of the traditional Huichol government in this region of the Sierra, in another day's trek.

Upon reaching the end of the line for the bus into the mountains, we walked the thin trail along ridges high in the mountains and eventually into the valley of the ceremonial center of Las Latas, one of the most remote and therefore *intact* ceremonial centers of the Huichol.

I had just spent many months living with my friends in Las Latas, but they were still a little surprised that I had brought a stranger with me that was not my wife. If Ines had been my wife there would probably have been no questions; my Huichol friends were always telling me that I needed a wife. But Ines was not my wife and she was unfamiliar to them and their ways. Nevertheless we were still treated like family and enjoyed a meal of delicious blue corn tortillas and beans made fresh by the women.

With no news from my friends about the whereabouts of Tayau, the next morning we headed off on the narrow trail through the mountains to Santa Catarina. Before leaving, some of my friends, including the kawitéro Eunicio, pressured me to accept a guide for the trek—a young man who knew all the terrain and was apprenticing as a marakáme. But I already knew the trail and didn't want to impose on him because it was a long hike there and back. In retrospect I should have taken their advice—not because of the risk of getting lost, but rather to avoid getting harangued by the Huichol sheriffs. The *topiles* were generally younger men serving their first cargo, or position in the government. They were basically in charge of keeping outsiders out of the Huichol Sierra and running errands for higher-level officials.

I don't imagine that my friends in Las Latas told the sheriffs of our arrival and our trip but someone, probably from the bus ride, had spoken to the sheriffs and halfway to Santa Catarina I could hear footsteps behind us and we were stopped.

The sheriffs were not at all happy that we were on their land and heading toward the main ceremonial site. But with the sheriffs there was another kawitéro from Pochotita that I considered one of my Huichol mentors, as we had previously made the pilgrimage to the peyote desert together and since then he had invited me to many ceremonies. He was an enormously important man although humble as a mountain goat. I kind of wondered why he was traveling with the sheriffs but our situation prevented my questioning this most respected elder. Traveling without a guide in the Huichol Sierra was a no-no. Luckily the kawitéro, who far outranked the sheriffs, held off the sheriffs and offered us a place in the shade alongside the path where we could share some of his water and tell him what we were doing there.

This was actually the last clear thing I remember before the pillory. I had a few vague memories after sitting down with him, but that was all.

As it turns out, I was not taken to Santa Catarina as I originally thought. Apparently the kawitéro had given us water laced with peyote (or maybe even datura or solandra) and then we were taken to the rancho of Jesús where I was put into the pillory. Some two years later, I found out that the kawitéro had us taken to Jesús because he spoke excellent Spanish and was accustomed to dealing with tewaris. He thought giving us over to Jesús was much better than leaving us alone with the topiles, and he claimed not to have known that Jesús was going to put me in the pillory.

In any case, I must have simply been having a psychoactive-induced vision that I was outside the kalliway in Santa Catarina because as I was walking up the steep trail from Jesús's rancho, and as my head started to clear, I realized where I actually was. Jesús's rancho was not far from my friend Tayau's (well, not far for Huichol who spend their whole lives walking in the mountains) and I demanded to have an explanation of what happened to me (at that point I didn't know Jesús or even his name).

"When we first met and I freed you from the pillory you were having a vision. If you were a Huichol I would have been able to see what you saw, but you are not Huichol, so tell me, what was it that you saw?" Jesús asked while gruffly handing me my pack and motioning me to follow him as he began to walk briskly off.

"Who are you and what happened to me?" I countered hotly.

Jesús stopped dead in his tracks and turning to face me he stood up straight and proud. "I am Jesús Marcilino de la Cruz Carillo, *juez* [judge] of this territory. You were delivered to me by your friend the kawitéro for your protection. I decided to punish you for coming here without an escort and bringing a stranger. Now you must appear before the council officials to decide what is to be done with you next."

"Wait a minute," I said in protest, while now noticing his official vara sticking out of one of his morals, which signified his official position in the government. "I just came out of a torture device that I was stuck in for god knows how long. Isn't that enough punishment? And where is the German woman, Ines?"

Jesús laughed at me long and hard. When he was finally through, he explained that I was in the pillory for about twenty-four hours (a slap on the wrist in his opinion) and that Ines had been taken to Santa Catarina by the topiles for questioning. Even though I was known and liked by many Huichol in the Sierra, I still had to stand before the council for breaking the law of traveling with strangers and without an official Huichol escort.

"You're lucky the old kawitéro likes you and convinced me to hold you only a short while. If it were solely up to me, I would have kept you for at least a week."

As Jesús turned to continue up the trail, he asked me again about my vision with the peyote. "Come on boy, you can tell me. I am good friends with the peyote spirit," he added in a jovial tone. I had no doubt in my mind that his man with colorfully embroidered depictions of peyote sewn onto all the clothes he was wearing did indeed know the peyote very well.

"I had a vision that I was in Santa Catarina and was being held outside of the kalliway. There were lots of people there and it seemed like a fiesta was going to begin."

"Is that so," the peyote shaman said as he stopped once again and turned to look at me with a gleam in his eyes. "That's very interesting. Here, have some *tejuino* and tell me more," he added while thrusting at me a jug he had stored in one of his bags.

Tejuino is a homemade corn beverage, quite sacred to the Huichol, but I immediately knew that his tejuino was also mixed with peyote, which is not uncommon. I had had the tejuino-peyote beverage many times before while working in the fields with the jicareros. It was usually very mild and is excellent at warding off fatigue and hunger, but just then I recalled that the water the kawitéro had given me must have contained an unusually strong amount of peyote or something else to have rendered me without concrete memories. I was very familiar with the effects of peyote and over the years had been on four pilgrimages to the peyote fields of Wirikuta with the jicareros of Tuapurie and Pochotita, on three private pilgrimages with Huichol family groups, and attended many Huichol ceremonies in the Sierra that included ingestion of copious amounts of peyote. So setting my trepidation aside as to how strong his tejuino would be, I reluctantly took a few swigs and handed him back the jug.

Jesús chuckled and after a large swig handed the jug back to me. "Come on pup, drink the nectar of our ancestors and tell me your story as we walk through this sacred land."

I took a couple more swigs and began to tell the shaman of my vision. Except in that moment I staggered and nearly fell on my face due to the enormity of what I had suddenly remembered. How could I have forgotten, until then, the complete vision? Holding on to his shoulders to stabilize myself, I recounted for him what I had seen.

I was back in Santa Catarina, in the pillory, even though I now knew that I had actually been in the pillory at Jesús's rancho and not at the ceremonial center. Having been to Santa Catarina many times before, I knew that even if there had been a pillory there in the past, I had never seen one there in current times. This realization made my legs give out and as I fell to my knees bent over with my hands in the earth, I remembered what Jesús was coaxing me to recount.

In the pillory, I could turn my head just enough to see a line of five bulls being guided by many men down the steep trail on the large hill close to the kalliway. The men were approaching me in their ceremonial clothing and seemed to be headed toward the old church. But why? The dust was thick as they passed by me and I choked hard, unable to wipe the dust from my nose or face without the use of my hands.

The men guiding the bulls and many of the townspeople following them were carrying Christian crosses and effigies of Jesus Christ. It was then that I finally realized what the celebration was about. It was Easter! How could I have forgotten? But it was then that I looked into the light and saw Mary, not Jesus. Mary turned her head in the direction of the church as if beckoning me to watch. The bulls were now all lined up in front of the church with marakámes, jicareros, and townspeople gathered around.

A group of younger men circled the first bull in the line and with swift precision tied his legs and dropped him to the ground. I looked up to Mary and to my dismay she looked down upon me with a serious gaze and conveyed to me her thoughts: I was just like the bulls. I was a sacrifice for the gods. My blood would spill right next to theirs.

In desperation I called out to Mary to save me. When I looked up at Mary once more she was gone but I saw a beautiful white dove fly away and into the sun. It was just then that Jesús had come and released me from the pillory.

I came to my senses again to find Jesús pouring water on my head and shaking me. "You have seen much that many others never will," he said in a somber voice. "The fiesta of *Semana Santa* [Easter week] is just starting today, which means you have seen in some ways into the future—the bulls will not be sacrificed for a few more days. You have also seen Mary, the redeemer. She must be one of your guides. Although, maybe the vision of Mary was your mind's way of seeing one of our female ancestors. We shall see about that later. The white dove is a manifestation of what the Christians call the Holy Spirit. It could also be a vision of an ancestor's *iyari* [heart soul]. We Huichol tune in to the knowledge of birds, mostly hawks, eagles, and macaws. The sacred white-tailed hawk of our ancestor Great-Grandfather Deer Tail is all white on the belly and the tail except for the tips. Seen flying above you, especially in the sun, he easily appears pure white. If you were Huichol I would say you were visited by Takútsi Nakawé, our Great-Grandmother Growth, mother of the ancestors, and by Tatútsi Maxakwaxi, Great-Grandfather Deer Tail, the singing marakáme.

"This is very surprising news indeed. Here I thought you might just be another deranged gringo searching for Don Juan* or free peyote. Now I can see that you have a special gift, and I can also see what the kawitéro saw in you. These special gifts must be nurtured. I bet that is the real reason the kawitéro brought you to me. He doesn't want to teach you himself because he's too old now and has many other responsibilities. He probably figured I'd be the best man for the job since I know a lot about tewaris."

Jesús turned to begin walking again. He was chuckling to himself like he knew something really funny but didn't care to share.

"What are you snickering about, Jesús?" I asked in a semi-harsh tone. "It's not very nice to laugh at people behind their back!"

Once again Jesús stopped and turned toward me. "I did not put you in that pillory to punish you. Torture has never been an effective form of punishment. However, suffering and torment, pain and agony, can be miraculous tools when they break down our pride to such an extent

---

*Don Juan is the main character in the books of Carlos Castaneda. The early books recount experiences with entheogens such as peyote. These hugely popular books helped spark peyote tourism in the 1970s.

that we are lain naked in front of our Gods. In this state we are open to vision and knowledge from levels of consciousness never attained or explored in everyday ho-hum states of awareness and perception. The trick is to learn to reach these levels of conscious perception without the need to suffer so much. The first way to begin doing that, especially for men whose self-importance is so thick that it's blocking up the access to the divine, is to crack open that dam. The pillory helped to crack you open. You let out some crap and let some light come in.

"Consider yourself cracked!" He added, still chuckling, "We can talk more about this later, but first, come on, let's go and get this business with the council finished so we can see what's going on with the fiesta."

Walking with Jesús through the mountains gradually calmed my agitated state after recalling my visions and being *cracked open*. By the time we reached the ceremonial center, my mind was clear but I was also slightly frightened about standing in front of the council, as I had never done that before. As we passed by the kalliway, the sacred round temple, I glimpsed the fire burning in the center and was immediately drawn to it. But Jesús held me by the arm. "I know you want to be with the sacred fire right now, but first we must clear up your situation with the council."

We entered through the low door of the governmental building, which was simply a short one-story, one-room, adobe brick structure. Jesús motioned me to sit on a bench near the front door. He made his way to sit in the middle of a large table across from where I was seated. At the table were many officials, who turned stern faces toward me.

The council apparently had many items to discuss. I sat there for nearly three hours as they debated many situations in the community. As their session seemed to be completing or maybe heading toward a break, with a nod from Jesús, a rather large and deeply dark-skinned Huichol rose from his seat and began speaking rapidly in a loud voice in Huichol while pointing at me repeatedly. I had almost no idea what he was saying, but it was clear he was not happy with my presence. When he had finished, there seemed to be a question-and-answer period among the council. My stomach churned as I heard the word *tewari* being spoken repeatedly while they talked about me.

Looking around I saw many other Huichol standing or sitting around the room and I was glad to see two of my friends. But when I looked directly at them, they either looked away or looked at me with vacant eyes. It was apparent that they had little power over the council. In a formal setting such as this one, Huichol let the elected officials do their jobs. Most of these officials hold a one-year term and many of the onlookers had been, or would be, officials themselves and out of respect would not interfere. However, I felt devastated that they would not speak up for me. They knew me and knew that I was not there for illicit reasons.

Finally, the large Huichol who had spoken first addressed me in Spanish. He was the current head of security for the people of Santa Catarina and questioned me about why I was there. I explained to him that I brought Ines with me to see them because she wanted to donate money toward one or more of their many social projects.

"But why do you travel our lands without a guide?" He retorted. "You know the laws!"

"I apologize," I replied meekly. "I thought it would be okay because I have visited here many times and I was looking for Tayau."

"So where is Tayau? Show me Tayau! He is not here but you are here!" he shouted loudly.

This man was obviously doing his job. I knew he was supposed to be acting this way. It was expected of him. I was also certain he knew that I knew Tayau and he had heard about the many times I had financially helped groups of Huichol to make the sacred pilgrimage to the peyote desert and other sacred sites—and that I was friends with many jicareros, marakámes, and kawitéros. But it didn't help how I felt in that moment. I wanted to crawl under the bench. Luckily a man sitting at the far end of the dark table leaned forward and I caught a glimpse of his face. I recognized him immediately as a most important and famous marakáme whom I knew and had previously traveled with to the peyote desert.

He addressed the council, saying, "Whether we like it or not, we all know the rules. Anyone who enters the ceremony peacefully cannot leave until it is over, even our own people. Maybe if our security was better we wouldn't be sitting here now."

The marakáme glared at the head of security and the young sheriffs in the room. With a stern pout on his face, he waved his hands in a gesture of dismissal to them and then looked toward Jesús and the other council members. Jesús fidgeted in his chair for a moment and then stood up.

"It is settled then. James and the German woman will stay for the fiesta. Many of us here know James or have heard of him. For myself, I believe he has come here on behalf of the spirits of this fiesta."

The head of security stood up with a frown as if to argue but Jesús rebuffed him with the rise of his vara.

"But!" Jesús added in a loud voice. "There will be no cameras. And the sheriffs will keep a close eye on them. The sheriffs will take their cameras and any other recording devices immediately."

This seemed to appease the council, and my part of the meeting was over. I was escorted out and as I left I perceived small grins on the face of Jesús and my friends, who were eying me intently. Ironically the head of security and the younger sheriffs were dumbfounded when they asked me for my camera. I gave it to them gladly but truthfully informed them that I didn't have any film. I actually wished I could have taken a picture of their puzzled faces as they tried to comprehend why I had brought my camera but no film for it. I had simply brought my camera with my other things out of habit but had no intention of photographing anything in the Sierra on that trip. They looked inside the camera and through my things. With that done, the head of security actually smiled at me and with a genuine laugh handed me back my camera. One of the things I love about the Huichol is their fluidity—one moment deadly serious, the next moment smiles and laughter. He actually patted me on the back as he walked away. Later, during the third or fourth day of the ceremony, I had a long and friendly conversation with him as we sat outside the kalliway in the sunshine. At the end of our conversation, he jokingly added that it was perfectly fine if I took his picture with my camera. Especially because I had no film.

 # Jesucristo

The old shaman Matziwa, the one who spoke up for me at the council meeting, greeted me warmly in the afternoon when I saw him outside the tiny store in the village that sold soda, beer, and other convenience items. Many of the Huichol that were around us were surprised that the old shaman actually hugged me (Huichol are not known for their hugging) and invited me to sit in the shade with his family and make offerings for the ceremony. The surprised Huichol obviously did not know I had helped sponsor Matziwa and his family to make the long trip to Wirikuta to find out why many of the children in their community were getting sick. Many of the superstitious Huichol blamed the illnesses on evil sorcery by a wicked marakáme, which is quite typical. Matziwa came back from Wirikuta with the answer and probably felt somewhat indebted to me because his fame and reputation were added to greatly by that. I was glad to take him up on his offer. To be seated with his family on the ground in the shade of a small veranda between the kalliway and the church elevated my status greatly with the people of the fiesta who didn't know me.

Matziwa's wife instructed me to make offerings and said that I could share the materials they had brought. Most of the materials—small square pieces of cut wood, beeswax, and different colors of yarn—were for the making of *nierikas*. The physical process of making a nierika is simple. Basically, a flat piece of wood is covered on one side with a thin layer of a special type of beeswax (*cera de Campeche*) and then one by one thin pieces of yarn are placed in intricate patterns as they are stuck to the wood. Many colors of synthetic yarn are used in modern times to create elaborate and vibrant designs but in ancient times the Huichol used natural fibers and dyes.*

After a few hours of making offerings with Matziwa and his family, Jesús came and took me to the kalliway.

"You have many questions," Jesús said to me while we both stared deeply into the fire. "It seems you did not know that our tradition included the betrayal, death, and resurrection of Jesucristo."

"That's true," I replied after a long silence, not taking my eyes from the fire. I was truly surprised at the size and importance that this fiesta had in the lives of people I knew to be aboriginal or pagan in their beliefs and who had held steadfast for centuries in not succumbing to the various missionary attempts of Catholics from Spain and other Abrahamic offshoots such as the Jesuits, Franciscans, and Protestants.

After another long silence, Jesús said simply, "I can sum it up for you in just one word: *silver.*"

Totally confused by his statement, I looked up from the fire to him. He was staring intently at me with shiny red eyes as the fire mirrored his soul.

"Silver," I repeated. "What does Easter have to do with silver?"

"Huichol have a long and glorious history, and the present isn't so bad either," he began speaking very formally. "We have retained and in some cases restored our traditions to that which sustains us: the rain, the corn, the earth, the fire, the sun, the deer, and all the other beings

---

*Huichol have become quite famous for their modern yarn drawings. This art form originated from the ancient tradition of making offerings to the ancestor gods. In my book *The Journey of Tunuri and the Blue Deer* you can see Huichol yarn drawings created specifically for the story by two Huichol artists, Casimiro from the ceremonial center of Las Latas and Maria from San Andreas. Casimiro's father is the most recently appointed kawitéro of the Santa Catarina temple district.

both seen and unseen that give us life. But if you think we have not also been influenced by other human events in our history you are mistaken. We have been dealing with the Europeans and their offspring for centuries. Since the 1500s they have been taking our land and trying to stick things into our heads."

Another long silence commenced as I tried to grasp what he was saying. As I turned back to the fire an image of the ancient church, just a few hundred yards away and so extremely out of place in these remote mountains (there wasn't even a priest), came to my mind. For some reason I had previously resisted asking my Huichol friends about the church. Maybe subconsciously I didn't want to know the answers.

I had the feeling Jesús knew what I was thinking when he suddenly said, "Miners and missionaries. That is what ties silver to Easter."

"I still don't understand."

Jesús pulled his chair a little closer to the fire and began speaking in a slightly different tone of voice. I had not yet heard him sing as a marakáme; each marakáme has a unique style and tone, but I guessed this new tone was closer to his chanting voice.

"The miners came before the missionaries. It was the greed for silver that spurred the missionaries to subjugate the 'Indians,' to try and corral us in their churches and so enslave us to their work in the mines. You do not realize this but the aboriginal people of this continent had a big hand in changing the whole world. Believe it or not, the Huichol and many other native groups helped to form the modern world you now live in. It was the silver mines that brought Jesucristo to the Huichol. In the Bible it is written that Jesucristo was betrayed for thirty pieces of silver, just as the Huichol and many other tribes were betrayed by the silver. The aboriginal people here and Jesucristo have much in common."

As Jesús spoke, it suddenly dawned on me that this man was not only a marakáme and the current judge of this indigenous community, but he must also have some sort of formal Western education. I wanted to ask him about this, but I kept quiet as he spoke.

"The Mexican cities that you travel through to reach us, Fresnillo, Aguascalientes, and especially Zacatecas, were all established in the 1500s out of the greed for silver. But the silver did not stay here where it belonged. It was sent to Spain and other parts of Europe. All that silver from this land changed the world. Who do you think mined all that silver? The aboriginal people, of course. The many Native tribes of this land were forced to work either in the mines or in other jobs associated with the mines. The mines popped up all over Mexico, not just in this part, and with the mines came Jesucristo and all the other saints and of course all the churches. The important thing to remember is that the silver from these mines eventually helped to create capitalism, our peso and your dollar, as a way of life. Silver now had more worth than land, more than animals, and that is the world we live in now. In the eyes of traditional Huichol and the kawitéros, the betrayal of Jesucristo for thirty pieces of silver was the very beginning of the capitalist Christian world we are now surrounded by. To this day, ninety percent of Mexicans are Catholic. We Huichol are like a small raft floating in a sea of Christians and money. How could we not be in some way affected?

"But the Huichol here in the Sierra have very little silver. Some of us sell our art or go to work in the tobacco fields to buy things like candles and cattle and soda for fiestas like this one—or to help pay expenses to travel to the sacred sites such as Wirikuta, which I have heard you have helped many of my people do."

After a short pause, Jesús continued.

"We live on our ranchos, farm our lands, and renew the cycles of life and the great events of our history with our ceremonies and fiestas. One of these great events was the coming of Jesucristo. We do not celebrate this like our Christian friends. He is not our savior. But as Huichol, we relate to the betrayal, murder, and resurrection of Jesucristo and celebrate in our own way. We honor the sacrifice that Jesucristo made for his people by sacrificing the bulls in the church. The blood and meat of the bulls gives life to the people and symbolically celebrates the renewal of the world. We recount the story of Jesucristo in the singing of the marakámes throughout the night in front of the church where the bulls are sacrificed and then butchered. We share the body [the meat] of the bulls with everyone and have a great celebration. That is one example of the way we have incorporated the teachings of the missionaries while not losing our identity or traditions."

While trying to digest what Jesús had just told me, I remembered my vision when the bulls were being led to the church. The only question I could think of in that moment was, "Why bulls?"

Jesús laughed and said, "Well for one thing, they taste good! Don't you like eating a nice steak?"

I laughed with him and he added, "The real reason is that we credit Jesucristo in bringing us many things we like including cattle, chickens, and sheep, which we didn't have before he came. He has given us many things for which we are grateful including cotton and eggs and lard for making bread. Jesucristo also brought us the silk ribbon that we use on our varas. In the ceremonies of Semana Santa the bull is the body of Jesucristo, not some silly little wafer the Catholics use in their communion. This flesh is the real body of Jesucristo, not just symbolism. We take this very seriously. These bulls are blessed and prayed upon before they are sacrificed on the altar of Jesucristo, Madonna Maria, and the saints, and every single bit of their flesh and bones and hide will be used in some way."

As Jesús spoke of the ribboned vara he held in his hands, it seemed as though he had suddenly thought of something else. When he finished speaking, he put his vara away and said that it was time to leave the kalliway and that I should go and finish my offerings because he had much to do also. I had a million questions I wanted to ask him but they would have to wait.

Walking back to where Matziwa's family was still sitting in the shade making offerings, I saw Ines with a group of women and walked over to them. She hugged me fiercely and then went back to what she was doing: stirring one of the large ceramic pots containing the sacred corn beverage for the ceremonies, which needed to be stirred constantly for many days as it simmered on hot coals. Ines's clothes were covered with dust and charcoal, and as she eagerly stirred the pot she told me that she was staying in one of the sacred rirrikis of one of the main cargo holders and that she had been working nonstop with the women making tortillas and tejuino. A big smile and a wink of an eye told me that she had found what she came looking for.

I was rather surprised to learn she was offered a place in one of the few rirrikis of the temple compound as these, to my knowledge, were reserved for high-ranking cargo holders. But the Huichol never ceased to amaze me and I didn't ask any unnecessary questions. Since Ines was obviously being well cared for, I could concentrate on the fiesta and what Jesús had shared with me.

Matziwa was not around when I got back to the shady area where the family was still busily working while laughing and joking as well. They good-heartedly made fun of the nierika I was making because I was having a really hard time getting the yarn to stick to the beeswax, something that they did with astonishing precision. Luckily one of the small girls came to my rescue and showed me that the reason my yarn was not sticking properly was that it was curling up. One needs to straighten out the fibers of the yarn after it comes off the round spool, otherwise it will want to curl back to the shape of the spool. After her kind instruction, I was able to make a few very decent nierikas that depicted my soul-felt offerings.

Later that afternoon, in a crowd of people in the main courtyard I ran into a friend whom I hadn't seen in a couple of years. He was the grandson of one of the old kawitéros that I had supported and traveled with to Wirikuta with their extended family. José was a very interesting and extremely energetic young Huichol. He spoke excellent Spanish and even some English. He was in his twenties and he and his brother were employed by the state government as Huichol police officers for the town of Mezquitic, the Mexican town closest to the ceremonial center of Santa Catarina. Along with Huejuquilla, these two Mexican towns are the main points of entry and exit to and from the Sierra and are where the buses that carry Huichol on the rough dirt roads start and end. Mezquitic is also where the closest office of the INI (Indigenous National Institute) was located. The INI, founded in 1948, was replaced in 2003 by the National Commission for the Development of Indigenous Peoples. Both institutions are funded and administered by the Mexican government, guided by their idea of how to "develop" indigenous cultures.

José was elated to see me, as I was to see him, and he invited me to come to his grandparents' house to visit, which was one of the only permanent homes in the ceremonial center. I was surprised and happy to see that the little dwelling was actually one of the low buildings on the other side of the courtyard across from the church and the kalliway. Having a home inside the ceremonial center was very prestigious as well as handy during multiday ceremonies. High-ranking people in the temple district, such as a kawitéro like Jose's grandfather, sometimes had houses in the ceremonial center apart from their ranches farther away in the mountains.

But my happiness at seeing José and going to visit his grandfather quickly dissipated as the memory of the pillory popped into my head. Standing outside the front entrance, I realized this was almost exactly the same place where I was put into the pillory in my vision—in the open area right between the old church and the kalliway. Jose noted my sudden change in mood and stared intently at me for a moment as though peering into my thoughts.

He then quietly ushered me into the tiny casa of his grandparents— a low-ceiling adobe structure with a front sleeping-sitting section and a back cooking area separated by a large piece of hung fabric. As I entered, Grandmother Paulina came out from the back and greeted me warmly, even though typically Huichol women won't even talk to tewaris. But Paulina is an elder, the lifelong wife of a kawitéro, and she is way beyond shyness or caring what other people might think. Plus I helped support the arduous trip for them to Wirikuta and spent weeks with them getting to the peyote desert, collecting the peyote, and engaging in all the intense ceremonies related to the pilgrimage.

After a few words with Paulina and my eyes adjusting to the semi-darkness of the windowless structure, I turned to see the old kawitéro resting on his low bed. Paulina announced to him that I was there, and I got the immediate feeling that his eyes had gotten worse and he couldn't see well. The last time we had been together a few years earlier, his eyesight was beginning to fail. This is actually common with both kawitéros and older women: women because they spend a significant part of their life sitting and standing beside smoky fires while cooking; kawitéros and marakámes due to a lifetime of ceremonies with the smoke from fire. Unfortunately the kawitéro Alejandro was also a chain smoker of a rustic form of tobacco.

"James, you've come back," Alejandro said sleepily but then immediately sat up. "Come. Come sit with me awhile before the ceremonies start." The old kawitéro motioned me to sit with him and we talked for hours about all kinds of subjects when finally he broached the subject of my specific reason for visiting the ceremonial center that time. I told him all that had happened, including my incident and vision in the pillory.

Paulina, overhearing our conversation, interrupted and added politely that it was time for Alejandro to get ready for the ceremonies. And then she did a most unexpected thing—she walked over to the small shelves next to the bed and produced a lidded glass jar about the size of a standard mason jar and handed it to me.

"This is the ground powder of some of the peyote you helped us collect and it has been prayed upon by this kawitéro and all our family. I want you to have it to aid in your time here and with the ceremonies. You deserve it, and from what I have overheard you will need the spirit of the blue deer and the ancestors in these coming days and nights to fortify you and gain clarity."

She handed me the jar and abruptly turned and went behind the fabric divider into the other area. I stood holding the jar, feeling both proud and slightly intimidated by this most sacred gift. Alejandro looked at me intently and asked me where I would sleep during my stay. When I told him I wasn't sure, he insisted I use his bed, saying that his responsibilities during the days of ceremonies wouldn't allow him to sleep. He would be chanting with the marakámes night and day. Caught by surprise by his generous offer, I accepted but had the feeling I wouldn't be sleeping much either, especially with the gift I now had from Paulina. One of the effects of ingesting peyote is that it keeps you awake for long periods of time even when engaged in extreme mental and physical tasks.

Leaving the house of Alejandro and Paulina, I almost ran smack into Jesús, who was walking by in the crowded area in front of their house at the same moment I was leaving. He stopped and looked at me with a bit of surprise but also a calm knowing. He glanced toward the entrance of the kawitéro's house and said, "Seems like you have some powerful friends here. You of course will be supporting the chanting of the marakáme Matziwa and his group during the ceremonies since you made your offerings with them. The kawitéro Alejandro will be chanting with a different group and also with the other kawitéros in the kalliway. Since it seems you have a good relationship with the kawitéro Alejandro and the kawitéro Eunicio, you will also be welcomed and expected to be supporting most all the groups. Right now I think it best if you come with me for a time."

Center of the Universe

We walked together again to the kalliway, and upon entering I was happy when Jesús brought me a *uweni* to sit in next to his. The uweni is a special chair that the marakámes and leaders of the current five-year ceremonial cycle sit on during certain activities inside and outside the kalliway. Whether inside or outside, a marakáme will almost always be seated in a uweni while he is singing in front of the grandfather fire. The uweni is a high-backed chair made of wood and woven reed with a deerskin border around the seat. The Huichol also make miniature uwenis as offerings for various ancestor deities to sit in and these are carried and left in sacred places on pilgrimages. Among all his other things, the marakáme of the last pilgrimage I went on carried an almost full-size uweni on his back from the Sierra all the way to Wirikuta and then all the way up to the sacred site on the mountaintop of Reu'unar where he left it in the rirriki as an offering to Father Sun.

"I am taking it upon myself to explain to you briefly the significance of the sacred temple in which we are now sitting so that you will better understand what is going on. Maybe you already know some of these things, but it is good that you enter into this place with a broader understanding.

"This circular temple with sunken floor and thatched roof is a replica of the universe. Here the underworld, Taheitxua; the middle world, Hixuapa; and the upper world, Taheima, are brought together and join with the five directions and where all the major ancestors are represented. Jesús took out a *muvieri* from his *takwatsi* and in the dirt floor he drew a circle with an equal-sided cross inside of it. The arms of the cross extended to intersect the circle. "This symbol shows you the most sacred places of Huichol. In the Center is Teakata, the birthplace of Grandfather Fire here in the Sierra. You have been there, right?"

"Yes."

"Good. Now in the West is Tatei Haramara, where the Mothers of the western rain come from and the Mothers of the ocean live. This place is on the seashore of San Blas in Nayarit. You've been there, too. Right? Good.

"In the East of course is Wirikuta, where there are many sacred places of springs and hills and where the sacred peyote grows and Cerro Quemado, or Reu'unar, where Father Sun first rose. You of course have been there, right? Good.

"Next is Tatei Xapawiyeme in the South where lives our Mother the rain from the south on the island in Lake Chapala. You've been there, right? Good.

"And in the North is Hauxamanaka, the Cerro Gordo [fat mountain] in Durango, the home of Maxakwaxi—Great-Grandfather Deer Tail. You've been there, right?"

I shook my head no, and Jesús responded immediately, "No! I am very surprised. You must go in order to complete the cycle, the circle. If you do not complete all five they mean nothing."

"I was never invited to go on pilgrimage to the Cerro Gordo," I replied.

"Well you are invited now! I will see that you make it there sometime. You will like it because there are no tourists there. It is our safest sacred place for that reason, well, beside Teakata here in our home. All the other places are getting spoiled by the Mexicans and need protection. Lake Chapala is contaminated, they want to build a port for ships

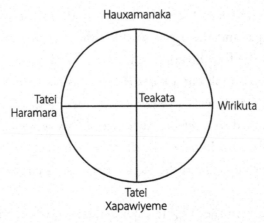

Five most sacred places of the Huichol

on top of Haramara, and Wirikuta is losing its peyote to poachers and farmers and is threatened again by new silver mines.

"Well let's get back to what we were talking about. You are not expected to memorize or learn all the names or significance of all the ancestors, as you are not Huichol, but it is good to know and hear about the major ones for now.* Each of these ancestors is incarnated for five years by one jicarero who represents his deity in all the ceremonies and pilgrimages, here in the kalliway, and in daily life working in the fields.

"Incarnating their deity is the main task of each jicarero. These ancestors include of course Tatewari [our Grandfather Fire], this kalliway is his house where he brings the three worlds together, Tayau [our Father Sun], Takútsi Nakawé [our Grandmother of Fertility], Tatútsi Maxakwaxi [our Great-Grandfather Deer Tail], Tatei Haramara [Grandmother of the Ocean], Tamatsi Parietsika [our Elder Brother Sunrise of the East], Tamatsi 'eka Teiwari [our Elder Brother the Wind], Tamatsi 'iriya [our Elder Brother's Arrow], Tatei Werika 'iimari [our Mother Young Eagle, the goddess of the sky], Kauyumarie [Peyote Deer], Watakame [Planter of the First Maize], Kamikime [Wolf Man], Ulu

---

*Over the years I realized that in different ceremonial centers some of the lesser deities differed slightly in name and function, but the main ones were always the same.

Temay [Young Star or Arrow], Nairi [Falling Rain], Tsakaimuta [Brings Deer], Kwixuxure [Red-Tailed Hawk], Tatei Ni'ariwame [Grandmother of Clouds and Messages], Tatei Kewimuka [Grandmother Rain that comes from the West], Tatei Yirameka [Grandmother Baby Maize], and Tatei Xapawiyeme [our Grandmother Rain from the South]."*

When Jesús had passionately listed these deities he rose from his chair and very carefully put some more wood on the central fire that was always lit whenever I had visited. With an intense look that seemed to conceal a grin he sat back down and said, "I can feel an energy from your moral [the embroidered Huichol bag I carried when with them] that is no doubt that of the hikuri [peyote]. I did not feel it before so I'm guessing you have acquired it since you arrived."

"Yes," I replied. "Paulina gave me a jar of ground hikuri from the pilgrimage I aided their family with last year."

Handing me a gourd cup† he said, "Take some of your powder and mix it with this water with my muvieri [feathered shaman's wand] and we shall drink the sacred nectar together here in the center of the universe."

I carefully did what he said and we both drank from the cup. Afterward he began speaking again while staring into the fire.

"The underworld from which everything grows is represented by the sunken floor of the kalliway and is connected to the other worlds by the small sacred holes [portals] in the floor, each of which is covered by a round sacred stone. In these holes, we place effigies of the ancestors of fertility and growth and also offerings to these life-giving deities. We also dance on the floor of the underworld to wake up the ancestors before planting and to call in the rains.

"The middle world in which we live is represented by the stone foundation of the temple, the deer antlers hung on the walls [which

---

*These are some of the main cargos for the jicareros that Jesús mentioned, but there are many more. Large temples such as Tuapurie will sometimes have close to forty jicareros.
†Halved gourds of various sizes are used both as ceremonial items—jicaras—and also as simple culinary bowls and cups.

represent specific deities], and the small recesses in the wall that hold the jicaras and offerings of the cargo holders."

Because the kalliway is lit only by the central fire and therefore usually quite dark, I had never noticed all the small recesses in the wall around the circular temple, but as Jesús was speaking, the darkness covering the walls seemed to lighten so I could see them more clearly. As I looked around the temple with new insight, Jesús peered at me knowingly with his now familiar grin and a glint in his eye.

He then continued, "The underworld, middle world, and upper world are physically connected by, and symbolically connected by, the two large pine posts that hold up the roof of the kalliway. These posts have many symbolic meanings but most importantly they deliver the rain from above to the soil below. The thatched roof is the sky, and in the sky we place five sacred plants: one in each of the four directions and in the Center."

I looked up and once again saw what I not noticed before. Indeed, tied to the ceiling, one in each of the cardinal directions and one in the Center, were small bundles of different kinds of plants. I also now noticed that on the two massive posts that held up the roof were tied the masks of several deer.*

Reading my mind Jesús added, "Yes, we bring the masks of certain deer to the kalliway so they can share with us the festivities and ceremonies. Since we honor them in this special way, they bring luck to the hunters knowing their relatives will be treated with respect and dignity."

At that moment I noticed someone else enter the kalliway, and it turned out to be Jesús's granddaughter Maria, who appeared to be in her midtwenties. Jesús introduced us and after a moment's hesitation said that he had something to do but that Maria and I should stay in the kalliway and talk. I was rather surprised at this because I knew it

---

*The Huichol will take the "face" off a deer killed on the sacred deer hunt by removing the skin, including nose, ears, and antlers, and then drying it to preserve the essence of the deer, making a sort of mask of the deer.

was rather unusual for a tewari to be alone with Huichol woman. It demonstrated that Jesús trusted me, but for some reason I got the feeling that he had ulterior motives.

With Jesús gone we both just sat there for a few moments not sure what to say but then it occurred to me to that I might be able to find out the answers to the some of the questions I had about Jesús. So I asked her politely.

"Jesús seems to be very knowledgeable about history outside of the Huichol Sierra and speaks almost perfect Spanish. How did this happen?"

"He has not told you himself?"

"No, and I haven't asked him. Is it okay that I talk to you about it?"

"Well, sure. It is not a secret. It is one reason he is elected to serve in many different positions for the community, especially those posts that deal with the outside world. My grandfather is very special. He is a great marakáme but he also knows a lot about what's going on outside the Sierra. My grandfather walks in many different worlds all at the same time. He knows many people on the outside and has traveled to many places. He is often asked for his advice."

"Can you tell me more? How was he educated?"

"Well, it started like this.* When we were very young there was a long drought in the Sierra and we had little food because the *milpa* [garden, cornfield] did not grow. Many people went west to the tobacco farms to work for a few pesos a day to buy food. But the tobacco has many chemicals and it is dangerous and backbreaking work. Some people that could make good artwork went to the coast to try and sell their art to the tourists in places like Puerta Vallarta and San Blas, which is near to our sacred site of Haramara. Our parents decided to take us to

---

*Oftentimes Huichol will tell an important story, or history, as if they were there even if they were not. Maria wasn't even born when this story happened but in listening to her you wouldn't know. She is invested in the story of this piece of history at so many levels she can actually relive it, in this case as Jesús's sister. Marakámes often do the same thing while chanting about history, creation, and tradition.

Guadalajara. Our parents are good artists and also some of my aunts and uncles. So we all went to Guadalajara. But most of us had never been outside of the Sierra. We did not know about life in a big city. Guadalajara is the second biggest city in all of Mexico. It is huge and stinky and crowded. There were some Huichol already living there and we found some. The people were living in old abandoned buildings making artwork and trying to sell them on the streets. So that is what we did too. It was very hard. We were always hungry. We were lucky to have just a few tortillas and maybe some beans each day. But the tortillas in the city are different than ours in the Sierra. The corn is not sacred and does not satisfy you like our tortillas."

"Yes," I interjected. "I have never tasted anything like them. Your corn is pure and very nutritious and without chemicals. The blue corn tortillas of the Huichol are my favorite. It fills my belly!"

Maria smiled knowingly and I asked her to please continue her story.

"Well, one day we were on the sidewalk with our art spread out for the people to see and a kind priest came by and he bought a few small things from us. During the next month or so he came by a few times. Sometimes he would buy a few things, sometimes not. One time he brought us some tortillas. But it was very hard for us living there and we were very unhappy. We are not city people. There are many different germs, too, and little Jesús became sick.

"One day when the priest came by he saw Jesús was sick and he was concerned. The next day he came back with some medicine, and later Jesús started to get better. Some weeks after, my parents decided to go back to the Sierra. My uncles did not want to stay in the city and neither did we. But the day before we were ready to leave, the priest came by and talked to my parents. He said that he was very worried about little Jesús because he was the youngest and he was so very thin and weak. He told my parents that he could take Jesús to his church where he could live at the mission in exchange for doing some odd jobs like cleaning and gardening when he got his strength back. He said Jesús would get three good meals a day at the mission, he would go to school, and be well taken care of.

"My parents were very desperate not knowing where we would get our next meal. But they did not want to give Jesús away. The priest said he was not 'adopting' Jesús. They could come back and get him anytime. One of my uncles was the only one that spoke Spanish good enough. Most of us did not speak Spanish at all, including of course little Jesús. So my uncle translated for my parents. My uncle thought it was a good idea to give Jesús to the priest because he said at the very least they would feed him and help him if he got sick."

"Did your uncle know the priest?" I asked.

"No, but he knew where the church was and the mission and the school. He told my parents in Huichol that he thought they had lots of money there and that they should give Jesús to the priest because maybe he would die if they didn't. So they did. I didn't see him again for many years."

"Do you know what happened to him during that time?"

"Well, yes, at least some things. My father and my uncle saw him a few times but they did not tell me or other people about Jesús. They would only say that he was doing fine and that's all. But when Jesús finally came home to the Sierra he told some things. At first his memory of that time when my parents left him was not good. He just said that he was very confused and scared. The teachers at the school did not speak Huichol so he was forced to learn to speak Spanish. At first he hated it, but then once he started learning he learned really fast. From what he told me, the priest kept his word and Jesús had plenty to eat, went to school, and worked at the mission helping out with things. But he did not like living there and he missed the mountains and his family and they made him wear the uniform clothes of the school.

"Once his Spanish was good enough, the priest gave him more jobs to do. One was to be an altar boy for the church. My brother learned all the words to the mass and all the songs and all the things to do. The priest also made him study the Bible every night and memorize many things. He was very demanding of Jesús, much more than with the other children. But for that reason he became even smarter than the other kids!"

"Did he begin to like it there?" I asked.

"He said he thought about running away but he had no money and didn't know how to get home. He said that sometimes in his dreams he was visited by the Mother Mary and she told him to stay and learn and when it was time he would be reunited with his family. So in secret he started getting books from the library to learn about things that the school didn't teach him. They of course taught him Mexican history and all sorts of other things like working with numbers, but he wanted to know more about his people so he found out a lot of things.

"One day he was making an errand for the mission and he found some Huichol on the street and began talking to them. He learned about all the different places where the Huichol lived throughout the city and began sneaking out of the mission to visit with them. He would mostly go at night when nobody would see him. He was happy to speak his own language and learned many things about his homeland and his people. But one day the priest saw him leaving and followed him. He got very upset at Jesús and punished him. He didn't tell me what the punishment was. But the priest talked to him for many hours about what he was doing and why. Then the priest forbade him to visit with his Huichol friends. Jesús said that he thought the priest had originally brought him to the mission as sort of a project. To see if he could make a Huichol into a priest!"

"Wow!" I exclaimed in surprise. "I had no idea Jesús had been through any of this. What happened next?"

"Well Jesús was very unhappy not to see his Huichol friends anymore and then the priest did something Jesús never dreamed of. He told Jesús that he was old enough now to start helping with the real work of the mission—spreading the word of Jesucristo. One day the priest told him they were going on a trip. He got on the bus the mission had and went with the others. But this was not just a trip. The priest sent him far away to another mission to live. He did not want Jesús visiting with other Huichol. It was somewhere in Oaxaca or Michoacán I think. It was an area with a lot of Indians but no Huichol. And aside from his regular jobs, he had to go with the adults and priests who were speaking to the Indians there about Jesucristo and the Bible and the church to turn them into *Cristos*. Jesús didn't want to do that. He had learned all about the church and the Bible but he was still Huichol. He didn't want to preach to people like the priests did about Jesucristo. He decided to leave and made a plan to get back to the Sierra. I don't know how he did it but he came back.

"When Jesús came back, our life in the Sierra was much better. The marakámes were singing well so there was enough rain and food. Everyone was happy that he came back. I'm sure there is much more to the story, but that's how Jesús began to know so much about the outside world. You can ask him more."

"So what did he do when he came back?"

"Well, that is the best part of his life, I think. He dedicated himself to learning everything about being Huichol. He has held cargo for the temple many times. Four times I think. Five years each time so that is twenty years of dedication. He got to know all the sacred places very well, especially Wirikuta. He was part of all the temple ceremonies for more than twenty years. I think he knows as much or even more than most of the kawitéros. The kawitéros are very old. Maybe Jesús will be a kawitéro when he is an old man."

"How did he become a marakáme?"

"Well, that is something you can ask him," Maria said strongly. "I know he has been singing the voice of the Grandfather Fire for many, many years. He knows all the ancient songs and histories. He does not drink alcohol like so many others do. He is a much-respected marakáme."

"You mentioned he has been to many places. How did that happen?"

"When Jesús was learning to be a jicarero, he also learned about making yarn paintings from our relatives. When our parents and relatives came back to the Sierra they met some German tourists that bought all their artwork. It was very lucky for us! Ever since then my father and my uncle, and later Jesús, stayed in contact and they still buy our art and sell it in Europe. We have a very nice connection with them. They invited Jesús to go visit with them in their country and he went all the way there! He has been there many times now and in other countries over there too. Last time he went to a country called Japan. I think he has also been to your country a few times. He doesn't have much time now to make his own art for sale, but he helps us selling what we make and we are doing very well."

"Would you like to visit other countries too, Maria?"

"Well, maybe someday you know? I have a lot of learning to do first. My path has been laid out in front of me so I know where I am going, but I have a long way to get there."

"I'm not sure I know what that means, could you explain about *your path*?" I asked sincerely.

"Well, first of all, I was born in Wirikuta. My mother was not supposed to go on the pilgrimage because she was so pregnant. But she had never been to Wirikuta and was afraid she would never get the chance to go. So she convinced Jesús to let her. She was fine the whole way there. But the day of the peyote hunt she gave birth to me. My grandfather says it was only a few minutes after they found and shot the first peyote with their arrows."

"Wow," I replied in surprise. "I was on pilgrimage once a few years ago and one of the women gave birth right there in Wirikuta just after we began hunting the peyote. Maybe you know her?"

A sad look came over Maria's face. "Is she from Tuapurie?" she asked.

"Yes, she's the sister of José, granddaughter of the kawitéro Alejandro. Their rancho is right near here."

"She's dead," Maria said calmly.

"Oh, my god, what happened?" I asked. This baby's birth in the middle of Wirikuta was one of the most incredible events I had ever experienced. On the pilgrimage I didn't even know she was pregnant. Huichol women are often rather rotund, and they always wear long dresses and blouses that reveal very little.

"Well, she killed herself because she could not live with the guilt, and she knew she would have a horrible life because of what she had done."

My mouth was hanging open and I was not even able to speak in that moment. So Maria valiantly continued. "Her and her husband were in the second year of their temple cargo. They were to be celibate—sexual relations only between the two of them. But she got pregnant from another man. She hid it from everyone. But when she had the child the secret came out. Maybe everything would have been better, but she did not confess having sex with that man or becoming pregnant. As you know, the confession in Wirikuta is very serious and sometimes can be life or death. In her case it was death."*

It was hard for me to wrap my mind around what Maria was telling me. I had just visited with her grandparents and spoken with her brother. I wasn't surprised that they didn't say anything to me about her death. Huichol are very private that way. But I was surprised that this all happened to a young woman who was a member of one of the most respected families in the Sierra. In any case, at that moment I wanted to get back to Maria's story so I asked her to continue.

"Well, thankfully I was born from my mother and father. They were also cargo holders when I was born but they were celibate. Because I was born in Wirikuta my grandfather and the kawitéros have always kept an extra-special eye on me to see if I would be a *cantador* [marakáme]. Of course for me there was never a choice. The great marakámes don't just decide to be marakámes. They are chosen. Jesús says that I was chosen and that is why I was born in Wirikuta. My mother was very early in delivery of me. Everyone thought that she would go on the pilgrimage and come back and then have me. But Jesús says the ancestors in Wirikuta were impatient to see me so they pushed me out!"

*To Huichol suicide is not a sin but rather a regrettable but acceptable way of ending one's life.

With both of us now laughing, I asked, "So your path is to be a marakáme?"

Maria sat up perfectly straight and in a more serious tone declared, "Someday I will be an exceptional marakáme, an expert weaver, a providing mother, and a faithful wife."

"Well, that's a mouthful!" Jesús declared as he re-entered the kalliway holding three very tall but thin white candles.

Jesús had us join him on the North side of the temple and gave Maria and I each a candle. In a mysterious voice he told me that I should light a candle for the ancestors of the North since I had never been in their presence and that I should request to visit with them. He added that both he and Maria would light candles with me in support. We lit and left our candles under the niche in the kalliway wall designated to Maxakwaxi, the main ancestor deity of the North.

The next couple days were filled with ceremonies. Some were clear to me as to their meaning and for some I really had no clue about their significance. At times I would ask my friends questions about what was going on, but mostly I just watched and was thankful for being witness to such a complex set of ceremonies and the chance to hear various marakámes sing.

After the fiesta of Semana Santa was over, Jesús invited me to come visit on his rancho, which was not far from the ceremonial center. He said his family was constructing a new rirriki to replace the old one and that an extra hand was always welcomed. I jumped at the chance to spend more time with the marakáme and his family.

The Gnosis of Jesús

One evening after working on the roof of the rirriki all day, we were casually sitting around while the women were preparing tortillas, and I told Jesús that I had spoken with Maria about him but wanted to know more about his experiences. I was especially interested in what happened to him after he left the mission.

"It was difficult for me when I first returned to the Sierra. Everyone had heard that my parents gave me to the priest and I was living at the mission. There were rumors that I had been turned into an *aleluya*."*

"Which means?" I asked.

"Aleluyas are what the Huichol call other Huichol who have forsaken their spiritual heritage and turned Christian. They are not permitted to live in the Huichol Sierra because they do not contribute to our culture. They no longer participate in our traditions that keep us in balance with the powers and forces that keep us alive. They don't listen to the guidance of the sacred peyote and the ancestors. They don't visit the sacred sites anymore, and they especially don't sing with the grandfather fire. In essence, once they devote themselves only to Jesucristo they are not really Huichol anymore—at least, not in their hearts."

---

*This word derives from *hallelujah,* which in the Christian church is often used as an expression to praise God.

"So your people thought you were an aleluya?"

"They didn't know for sure. But they knew I lived with the Christians for many years. I went to church almost every day and studied and memorized the Bible. I was taught how to be an altar boy. I went to their school, wore their clothes, and ate their food. I had no way to engage in my ancestral spirituality or culture. But even with all that, I never forgot who I truly am. I am Huichol. My heart lives in the Sierra. My genetic code is infused with the sacred sites, the corn and deer and peyote."

"So you turned your back on all you learned from the Christians?"

"I wouldn't put it exactly that way. I have respect for most of the moral teachings of Jesucristo, the core is the same as other great religions. But I do not live my life for Jesucristo and I don't agree with many of the actions of the church. Looking back on my years living with the Christians I can see that they helped me to open my eyes to who I really am, and also they provided me with many tools and knowledge that I still use today. For that I am grateful. How does the saying go . . . I have tossed out the bathwater but kept the baby!"

We both laughed as Jesús caught me off guard with his articulate wit. "I have felt a similar way while moving away from my Catholic upbringing," I responded.

"That's probably because in your heart you believe in *gnosticismo*. As do I."

"I'm not sure what you mean?"

"It's very simple," Jesús replied. "The central idea of gnosis is direct knowledge of the spiritual world, not simply faith in some religion or someone else's written word. Huichol and gnostics indeed gain knowledge from other people but they crave and seek their own personal experiences. They do not rely on others to tell them what is true or what to believe. And above all, they do not try and force or coerce others to believe what they do. There are many things I can show you to help you learn about how to become a mature being, but I believe the only path of spiritual knowledge, connection, and enlightenment comes through direct personal experience. For that reason, I would never say to you that you must follow my teachings or the teachings of the church or else you will burn in hell—that there is only one true religion or spiritual path. For me, the people that say that are demonstrating how naive they are. A truly wise person relies on his own experience and knowledge."

"I agree with that," I said earnestly. "But I'm surprised you use the term *gnosticism*. I am certainly no expert on the subject, but I thought that gnostics seek to transcend the details of physical life. I see very little of that in you. And to be honest, I never would have dreamed of having a conversation about gnosticism with a Huichol."

Jesús laughed merrily. "Yes, yes. You are correct. I am a man of this world. But I am also a man of other worlds. It is a tricky subject. Let's put it this way: I have learned to place my consciousness into realms outside of my body. But I am not trying to escape my body or my Mother Earth. I am also not trying to dominate the Earth and all beings, like the modern followers of Jesucristo and both of our governments. I desire to be one with all, whether here in this physical realm or in other nonphysical dimensions. In the strictest sense I guess you could say I am both a Christian heretic and a gnostic heretic. Although, the Greek word *heretic* literally means 'able to choose, to think for oneself,' so maybe it's best to simply call me a plain old heretic. I like that. The churches condemn those who don't follow like sheep and say that those who don't follow are committing heresy because thinking for oneself is not allowed. That makes you a heretic, too!"

I must have had a puzzled look on my face. Jesús continued.

"Look at it this way," he said. "And correct me if I'm wrong. You mostly feel at home in your physical world. You enjoy the immediate experience of connecting with plants and animals, the sights and sounds of the seasons, and the weather. In most cases, you feel satisfaction in physical work and you are not opposed to the physical pleasures of sex. To you, all these things are sacred. However you also know there is more. You learn techniques to alter your everyday consciousness and partake in sacred plants like the hikuri to explore different states of perception and awareness. Your spiritual quest includes both magnificent earthly experiences and also journeys into the numinous nonphysical realms. As a result of decades of actual experiences with all of these realities, you tend to not allow people to tell you what to believe, what is real and what is not, what is capable or incapable. In a nutshell, you have learned to think and act for yourself—to make your own decisions. You, my friend, are the definition of a heretic. That's why we get along so well together. The life of the heretic is the only path for us!"

"Well, when you put it that way, I guess I am a heretic. I do think for myself and make my own decisions. And I don't let other people tell me how or what to think. But isn't that relative? I mean at some level everyone makes their own choices. One can ultimately decide to be Christian or Muslim or Jew or Buddhist or agnostic or heretic or anything else."

"Sure," Jesús replied while shaking his head. "But you're missing the point. We were talking about aleluyas and Christians and why I left the mission. The aleluyas and Christians decide to buy in to the institution of the church. Huichol don't go to church mainly because it takes away the freedom to think for yourself. To be a true Christian of the church you must commit yourself solely to the teachings of the Bible or suffer eternal damnation. Period. There is no other road. They have accepted that as true. I cannot accept that. Especially when the 'good book' was compiled in order to control people. The New Testament, the cornerstone of modern Christianity, is incomplete and misleading. People have decided to put all their faith in a book! A book that is not even accurate! That book was assembled to create the institution of the church. Men that wanted control of the people decided what to put in and what to leave out. Jesucristo didn't. Men did."

"Yes, well, the gospels were written by the apostles about the life of Jesus, not by Jesus himself," I added.

"Actually, the gospels were not even written by the apostles. They were written by others *in the spirit* of the apostles, or maybe by *divine intervention*. The church fathers said "Mark wrote this and John wrote that." But they didn't. And to me it doesn't really matter except for the fact that I don't like to be lied to. I personally much prefer divine intervention. But the point isn't so much that the New Testament wasn't written largely by who is claimed to have written it, so much as who decided what it contained and why. There were lots more books and letters, what are now called *gospels,* floating around at the time the Bible was formed. The Gospels of Mathew, John, Mark, and Luke were only four of many. The New Testament was formed from these because of the significance of the murder and death, and especially the resurrection, of Jesucristo."

"So why would the church leave out the others?"

"Like I said, they wanted control. They wanted everyone to believe that Jesucristo came back to life in his physical body, and that only the eleven apostles that witnessed the resurrected Jesucristo had the authority to lead the Christians after Jesucristo left the Earth. For two thousand years now, Christians have bowed to this single view of authority: the apostles held authority and their successors are the bishops and priests who carry on the authority. The pope himself traces his authority to Peter, the first apostle, the first to witness Jesucristo resurrected."

"So you're saying that the church leaders edited the New Testament to gain authority over the people. Interesting."

"But that is only part of it. There were people then and still today that discount the so-called authority of the apostles. Among many other things, they note that Paul, the author of more than half of the books in the New Testament, never even met Jesucristo! Paul was originally a Jewish killer of Christians. He never met Jesucristo, he never had dinner with him, he never even heard the voice of Jesucristo. Jesucristo came to him on the road to Damascus in a supernatural vision! He *converted* into a Christian and through his ministry, building of churches, and writings, is considered one of the most important figures in Christianity.

"The point being that there are those who believe the resurrection of Jesucristo is not a literal event in the past as much as a spiritual message in the present. As for Paul, the author of more than half of the Christian Bible who never even met Jesucristo, they say that Jesucristo appears in visions, and also in dreams and trances. This goes directly against the authority of succession from the apostles to the bishops and priests. If anyone may encounter the risen Jesucristo, the authority of the church means nothing! Imagine also that there are those who say Mary Magdalene was the first to see the resurrected Jesucristo and that the others didn't see him until later. Oh boy! A woman? The first apostle? That certainly doesn't sit well with a church that does not even allow women to be priests."

"So you're saying that there were Christians who believed they could see the resurrected Christ for themselves? Like Paul and Mary? That sounds more like gnosis than religion."

"Exactly! The gnostic Christians have always argued against the institution of the church because of the authority to claim universal [Catholic] ownership of the Christian religion. The gnostics disregard such authority. Their position is that whoever comes into direct personal contact with the numinous—whether it be God, Jesucristo, the Holy Spirit, whatever—experiences the ultimate truth. Secondhand knowledge and traditions are subordinate to direct experience and therefore religious authority cannot be institutionalized."

"Sounds kinda like the Huichol I know," I said.

"You got that right. For both Huichol and gnostics, spirituality must be fluid, spontaneous, natural, adaptable. Sure, we Huichol have lots of traditions and rituals. But they are not static. They are like running water, not a stagnant puddle that has sat there for two thousand years. We adapt to the world we live in while still bearing in mind the teachings of the ancestors. Listen closely to what I just said. The teachings of our ancestors. Not the authority of our ancestors. This is the difference between Huichol and gnostics and the church. But do you know this only scratches the surface of why both aboriginal people like the Huichol and ancient and modern gnostics were driven away from the church? There are two very powerful situations having to do with consciousness that are rarely spoken about by those that the church calls *los laicos*. You know what that means, right?"

"I think you are talking about the laity, which refers to the common people of the church. Not the bishops and priests—the regular people."

"Yes, yes. You could also call them sheep as opposed to the shepherds who are the clergy. You can also call them nuns because even those women who devote themselves to poverty, chastity, and obedience to the church are still only part of the laity. They can never be clergy. But back to the two points. The first one is very important because it deals directly with multiple gods. As you know, there are religions throughout the world, including those of aboriginals, that honor or pray to multiple gods. This of course is strictly forbidden by the Christian church. But did you know that there were early Christians who believed in more than one god?"

"No, I didn't. That sounds like heresy to me. I can't imagine that someone who believes in Jesus Christ would believe in more than one god."

"Ha-ha! Yes, it's hard to believe but it's true. This is a big reason the gnostics were thrown out of the church. The gnostics said to themselves, hmm, why would God say 'I, the Lord your God, am a jealous god . . . You shall have no other gods before me'? If there is only one god, then who was this God jealous of? Some gnostics believed that the God of Israel, the God of the church, was not the highest or supreme or even only god. They believed that the *creator* was a lesser divinity—or a single emanation of the supreme God—that created mankind. This *demiurgo* [demiurge] is sometimes referred to as malevolent, but some gnostics considered the demiurge to simply be flawed. His imperfect creation was not due to a moral failing but evidence of his ignorance and immaturity in contrast to the supreme God. Evidence of this consists of mankind's worst issues, which are unique to man, such as torture, lies, corruption, racism, tyranny, fascism, overpopulation, landfills, et cetera. These gnostics believed that the supreme God, the true God, the spiritually nonmaterial God, could never have intentionally created a being capable of such atrocities. However, the demiurge, not being inherently evil, also gave mankind the spark of light that is the essence of true God."

"But the church could not accept that position."

"Nope. And the main reason for that is simple. The gnostics claimed that through esoteric teachings one could be initiated into a higher form of spirituality than offered to the masses by the church. To them, the church leaders worshipped a lesser god, the creator God, the demiurge, and they, in contrast, were in direct contact with the supreme highest power—God the Almighty. The concept and worship of multiple gods by the ancient Sumerians, Egyptians, Greeks, Romans, Chinese, and Celts predated the Jews' and Christians' one-god theory so this certainly wasn't anything new. But what was new was that a believer and follower of Jesucristo could put their faith in a god different from the Christian church. Talk about heresy! These gnostics not only condemned the authority of the church—the bishops, priests, and deacons—as being immature and worshipping a lesser god, they considered themselves to be much more spiritually mature. They saw the clergy as representatives of the demiurge God, whom they have spiritually surpassed and so, therefore, have also surpassed the authority of the church."

"So they saw themselves as better than the clergy."

"Well, sort of yes. I guess they were kind of pompous. They acknowledged that the clergy, acting as agents of the demiurge, had legitimate authority over Christians who were not initiated in the gnostic esoteric teachings. That would include almost all Christians. But those followers of Jesucristo who were initiated and released from the control of the demiurge were now believed to possess a much higher spiritual authority—from the true Father and Mother, the true God. The jealous demiurge God was likened by these gnostics to the jealousy of the bishops toward those Christians they could not control by their threats. The inappropriate acts of the clergy—the ridiculous hierarchy of the church, the exclusion of important gospels and texts from the New Testament, the sexism toward women, the condemnation of other Christians who did not exactly share their views, among many other issues—pointed these gnostics to the conclusion that the clergy were a bunch of unqualified, uninitiated, blind followers of a grossly immature God. The early church fathers realized that their authority would always be challenged if they did not do something to squelch this so they came up with the Christian creed that clearly appoints their God as both father *and* creator. By their authority they banned the gnostic Christians from the church with this creed: I believe in God, the Father Almighty, creator of heaven and earth."

"So if the gnostic Christians were right, why are the Christian religions, the Catholics and the Protestants, by far the largest in the world but you never, or rarely ever, hear anything about gnostics?"

"Well, the best I can say about that is that maybe the early church fathers were as spiritually immature as the gnostics claim; I really don't know and I won't judge them, but one thing they were definitely not, was stupid. They understood very early that their church would not only survive but flourish if they could unite the Christian churches from around the globe and form them into a Catholic [universal] religion. They did this very efficiently and effectively. They were experts at marketing!

"Above all, the church wanted members, especially *paying* members, so they made it so that in order to be a member all you had to do was declare the creed, be baptized, go to church, and obey the clergy. Simple. On the other hand, the gnostics had strict criteria to establish spiritual maturity for anyone admitted to the *true* church. These gnostics cared not for obedience to the clergy or even baptism. Their mode of criteria was the level of understanding between what is true and what is false and the fatherhood, motherhood, unity, and wisdom that arises with gnosis—personally experienced knowledge. Many years might be spent in teaching select students before they were admitted. These 'secret' teachings were verbal and not written. The gnostics believed that anyone can read a book but that it took discipline and sincere longing to acquire gnosis. So as with other higher levels of spiritual teaching, the gnostic path appealed only to a few when compared to the Catholic Church, which appealed to the masses."

"But what about Jesus? Weren't these gnostics also Christians?"

"Yes, these were gnostic Christians; this is where it gets really interesting and leads to the second point I mentioned. These Christians had a very different idea about Jesucristo than the orthodox Christians of the church. They believed that Jesucristo came to save us. But not from sin . . . from ignorance. Ignorance is the cause of suffering. Knowledge is salvation. That is the gnostic Christian creed. Knowledge derives from personal experience, from gnosis. Ultimate knowledge is then found in the spark of the Forefather that lives inside us. In this way the gnostics proclaim that true knowledge of the self is true knowledge of God the Forefather. And because most people, including those of the church, are unaware of their own *selves* they live in ignorance and deficiency. Self-ignorance is destructive. It causes people to walk around asleep to their true nature like a sort of unconscious drunkenness. Jesucristo knew this and tried to change them. Unfortunately after he left the Earth the church edited a large part of his teachings to suit their needs. In one of the gospels that did not make the final cut of the New Testament, Jesucristo clearly admonishes the state of humanity. He says when he came into the world 'I found they were all drunk. None of them were even thirsty . . . they are blind in their hearts and do not have sight . . . empty they came into this world, and empty they seek to leave this world. But for the moment they are drunk.'*"

"So you're saying that the Christian gnostics believe Jesus came to teach us self-awareness?"

"Awareness, knowledge, mindfulness, wakefulness. However you want to say it. The big point here is that Jesucristo did not come here simply to die for our sins. That's just silly. He came to enlighten us to the gnosis of the Forefather God and release us from the demiurge. But this is not a simple task for anyone. It requires a more or less solitary process of inner self-discovery. It is much easier to simply remain asleep or stay drunk. That is why the Catholic Church prevailed over the gnostic Christians. The Catholics say they can simply confess their sins to their God through a priest and be saved. A gnostic has no priest and must find God him-

---

*From the Gospel of Thomas 38:23–29 in *The Nag Hammadi Library,* 121.

self, the hard way. In this way the gnostic Christians found Jesucristo as the exemplar: He was a homeless wanderer who rejected his own family and avoided marriage and having children all in the name of truth at all costs, even death. The followers of Jesucristo had to give up everything as well to be allowed to join him. This meant no job, no home, no family, no money. In the Gospel of Luke, Jesucristo says that whoever 'does not hate his own father and mother and wife and children and brothers and sisters, yes, even his own life, he cannot be my disciple.'*"

"I never really thought about it that way. That doesn't sound like much of a church congregation."

"Well, that's what the gnostics thought, too. And even beyond that, they held that Jesucristo was the model for their own esoteric method of teaching. Jesucristo masked his teachings in parables to the masses and truly taught only those whom he considered able to receive his knowledge. In the Gospel of Mark he says to his small group of followers, 'To you has been given the secret of the kingdom of God, but for those outside everything is in parables, so that they may indeed see but not perceive and may indeed hear but not understand, lest they should turn and be forgiven.'† This was how the gnostics viewed spiritual teaching. If you are not ready or prepared for knowledge it will remain obscure. To those who have the burning desire and discipline to find out and know more about the true God, more will be given. Those who are *outside* are close-minded, asleep, prejudiced."

"So, Jesús, as a Huichol marakáme heretic who knows a heck of a lot about Christianity, what do you believe about Jesus Christ?"

"Ha, ha, ha! I have no beliefs about Jesucristo, you silly boy!"

"What? Come on, you of all people should have some opinion!"

"I have no beliefs and I have no opinions because . . . get ready . . . *I . . . am . . . Jesucristo!*"

I sat there with my head in my hands for a minute or so while

---

*Luke 14:26.
†Mark 4:10–12.

listening to Jesús laugh and chuckle at my exasperation. Finally I looked up at him, "What the hell does that mean?"

"Oh, lighten up," he replied. "I am Jesucristo, so get over it."

After a few moments and a couple deep breaths I replied, "Fine, I am light as a feather. Now, Jesucristo, could you please tell me what you mean by that?"

"We have been talking for some time now about this concept of gnosis. Direct knowledge of the spiritual world through personal experience. You happen to be talking to a Huichol marakáme whose whole world revolves around gnosis. But my gnosis is sometimes so intense, like that of the most intense Christian gnostics, that I *become* my gnosis. I see you are confused, so I will try and explain. The gnostic Christian who achieved gnosis was no longer a Christian. He or she became a christ, "christ" of course being a metaphor for becoming the light of God. Jesucristo, in the eyes of the gnostic Christians, was a pure emanation of the Forefather. Not the demiurge God of the church. With much work of self-discovery, they found inside themselves that spark of the Forefather and became as Jesucristo himself. In that same way you could say that I am Jesucristo. I have seen, experienced, and lived what Jesucristo was—the light of the Forefather. I am also the spark of the Forefather in the emanation of Tatéwari, Tayau, Tatútsi Maxakwaxi. I am all these things and many more.

"If you want, you can become Jesucristo, too," he added in a serious tone.

"No thanks. I'm fine."

"Oh, but you are not fine, you are like sleepwalking. If you find your spark, you can wake up. You can be whatever you want. If not Jesucristo, how about Buddha or Mother Mary or Krishna? You could be one of the giant sequoia trees that you love or maybe a condor or a tiger?"

"I think that for right now I'd just like to be me."

"Good answer! Let's see if we can find him!"

The Five Points of Attention

The next day, I was sitting alongside Maria outside her little house watching her do her weaving when Jesús appeared and said cryptically that I was being summoned by the ancestors to Teakata. We left immediately.

The hike to the physical center of the Huichol world is not very far from the ceremonial center of Tuapurie—I'd estimate three to four miles. But around Tuapurie are deep gorges with narrow, rocky trails that make walking difficult and strenuous. However, physically climbing down into the *barranco* of Teakata was the least of my worries because the closer we got the more I began to feel ill—not in my body but in my mind. This did not happen to me the first and only other time I had been there. On that occasion, I was visiting the community of Pochotita at the time the kawitéro was taking the people to Teakata to change the roofs of the many little rirrikis of the ancestors. Teakata, from what I know as a tewari, comprises caves and shrines of the most important ancestors (*kakayeri*) including Tatewari, Nakawé, and Maxakwaxi.

As I gazed into the gorge containing the most sacred place of the Huichol, I felt like turning around and running away as fast as I could. Jesús noticed this and firmly grabbed my arm and asked me what was wrong. I told him I didn't know but that I didn't want to go to Teakata.

"You have become much more sensitive since the last time you were here," he said in a concerned voice. "This is probably why we were summoned here. I believe it is time for you to have a very big lesson. Let's not go down yet."

Jesús led me a short distance away, and we sat on the ground of the mesa above Teakata where he began a formal instruction. He started by telling me that now that I was more sensitive to the powers of the iyari of the ancestors, I needed to know how to handle myself correctly. According to Jesús, Teakata was the perfect place to begin my instruction due to the fact that it was the center of the five sacred points of the Huichol universe.

"To touch the spark of God within you, you must start by nurturing your true being, your *esencia* [essence]. You see, you have three important parts that make up your *self*. You have your inflated ego—I am this and I am that. You have your essence—this is your true being that you were born with. And you also have your personality—the acquired characteristics of James. Aside from your physical body and eternal soul, in this life you are basically your ego, your essence, and your personality. Your ego is the trickiest subject but we cannot work on fixing it until we learn about essence. We have to work on our true *being*.

"Pay attention to this: We are born with our true being, our essence, which grows within us during early childhood. But modern man, industrial man, their essence ceases to grow after age three to five because the ego and personality are the ones nurtured by parents, school, job, relationships, et cetera. The essence has no place in the busy lives of modern people so it becomes stagnant and malnourished. I have seen that for people like you—Americans, Mexicans, Europeans, and other cultures that follow similar ways of life—there are usually only two stages of growth in life: the growth of the essence as little children and then the growth of the ego and personality until death. Do you know why you come to the Huichol and other aboriginal people to learn? I will tell you the truth. It is because our culture not only allows but encourages the essence to grow equally with the ego and personality. You can feel that very clearly when you are with us. Even though we don't have the level of intellectual knowledge of the dominant culture, our culture and people are in many ways much more mature because we have nurtured our essence throughout our lives. For you and for people of your culture, your continued growth as human beings will be the growth of your essence, which has been left behind. This is the third stage of growth for you."

"So you're saying that my essence doesn't grow naturally as I get older, wiser?"

"Older, no. Wiser, maybe. That depends on what you call wise. Inner wisdom of one's true self, yes. Knowledge as in books, computers, jobs like carpentry, banking, office work, no. You see, our essence doesn't naturally grow in time. Time is no factor. I know teenagers in the Sierra that know their essence more than any seventy-year-old man I know living in the city. What I am saying is the quality of life is much different. You and I both have what can be called book knowledge. You probably have a lot more than me. But as much as we can know about words and mathematics and science and philosophy and even the Bible, all of this, except for what we are truly gifted at, has nothing to do with our true essence.

"Man was born with two legs and feet for a reason. To walk! To explore the mysteries and beauty of nature. And our essence is tied to that which gives us life—sun, water, wind, fire, earth. Our essence is also what lives inherently inside each one of us, which should be nurtured, our specific gifts and talents. Our essence is also our inner quality, our level of being, our innermost values. But most of all, our essence asks us to seek the largest questions of the human being—What is the meaning of my life? Who am I? Where did I come from? Where am I going? When people live their lives centered on the ego and the personality and the intellect, at the expense of the essence, they are in disharmony just as someone who has developed their essence with no thought to personality, like someone trapped on an island alone their whole life, will be equally imbalanced. Harmony between essence, personality, and ego opens the door to true self-knowledge and the light of the divine."

"How do we go about achieving this balance?"

"Ha! Now you are starting to ask the interesting questions! Okay. First it is important to understand that we are all different beings. I am different from you. We are both different from a tree or a bird or a dog. Each is its own being. In your case, to better know your being you must elevate those parts of you that are lacking in harmony with the rest of your organism. For you and for most people like you, that means first working directly with your essence. Your essence has been stunted by your culture. But it's still there. It just needs to be brought out and nourished. Your essence needs to catch up with your knowledge."

"I'm not sure what that means."

"Think of it this way. Your essence has two tracks running parallel. On one track is the train of knowledge and on the other track is the train of being. All that you *know* is on the train of knowledge. What you truly *are* is on the train of being. When humans develop in balance these two tracks are built simultaneously. The construction workers even help each other to get the tracks built. But if one crew is not given enough materials then the tracks won't be even. One crew will be left behind. That train will stop as the other keeps moving.

"It is often the case for modern people that the train of knowledge has left the train of being far behind. The train of knowledge is valued much more in your culture. Is it not so? I have met many men who have lots of knowledge in words and science and are very well respected. But they can also be very selfish and cruel and conceited. And they are not in the least ashamed of their lack of development and the stunted growth of their being. On the contrary, most don't even realize their state of imbalance, and if they do they really don't care. Everyone around them in their culture acknowledges their grand knowledge but not their low level of being. They say, 'oh, he's just rude' or 'don't mind him, that's just the way he is.' But do you know that they would be much happier, more fulfilled, more mature, and more content with life if their true essence were allowed to shine out through the veil of knowledge?

"In this regard I see very little point in the accumulation of knowledge at the expense of our essence. What happens when the essence is lost is that we forget who we really are. To be mature human beings, we need to remember our essence. We are not simply creatures of books, computers, and scientific ideas. We are little gods that with some effort can live deep, fulfilling, and joyful lives.

"You are not Huichol, so in some ways getting in touch with your essence will be a different process than ours, but in some ways it will be the same. The culture we grow up in certainly has influence on our ego and personality, but we are all born as pure essence so at the core we are very much alike. Since I am a Huichol marakáme, I'm going to explain some things to you in the Huichol way. But since I am in some ways also familiar with your culture, I will attempt to describe things to you in a manner that makes sense, always keeping in mind that words are just words. Until we experience something we can never truly know it.

"You see, Huichol do everything in fives. That is our sacred number. Other cultures have other numbers, usually odd numbers like three or seven. For us it's five. We have five directions, five points of attention, five functions, five-year cycles as a jicarero, et cetera."

Jesús picked up a thin stick and in the dirt he drew a circle with an equal-sided cross inside it, just like he did in the kalliway, with the arms of the cross extending to intersect the circle. "What I am about to share with you is not something that Huichol usually teach each other because most Huichol, especially jicareros, marakámes, and kawitéros do this instinctually, naturally, and as a course of living in our culture. But it was spelled out to me this way by an ancestor spirit when I was becoming a marakáme.

"This is a valuable symbol for remembering the importance of five, which is core to bringing forth your true essence. Here we have four points where the cross meets the circle and a fifth point in the center intersection. In this way you can see that the five points are all connected. One of the many things this symbol represents is the five points of *attention*. To remember who you really are, you must consciously divide your attention. In the beginning this is not easy. It takes deter-mination, patience, and perseverance to become proficient.

"Is it not true that you have already had experiences in spitting your conscious attention?"

"Yes. Well, I think so."

"Well that is good and bad. It is good if you can hear what I say without analyzing or comparing to what you already know. To think that you already know would be bad because much of what I have to tell you, I'm sure that you don't know; but you might think you know and if you think you already know, then you won't really hear me. What I'm saying is that there may be a case where you have experienced something similar. That's fine. But don't let your past experiences close you to learn-ing new things just because you may think you already know them.

"It is a human habit that when someone is explaining something to us, but we have already done it, maybe even thousands of times, all we hear is blah, blah, blah, because we already think we know about it. Many times we even think we know more about something than the person explaining it to us. And maybe that is true. All I am saying is that there are an infinite number of ways to accomplish things, and if you pay close attention you may even learn more about something that you already think you know about. Do you get what I'm saying?"

"Sure. It's hard to keep your mind focused when someone is trying to teach you something that you already know, or think you know, or even know better than they do. I hear that. In this case I'm going to consider your instruction like an advanced course. Like a couple years ago, I took a course on bow hunting even though I have been bow hunt-ing my whole life and am very good at it."

Jesús sort of rolled his eyes at me. "Well, that will have to do, I guess. Besides, if you don't pay attention, that's your loss not mine. I'm only doing this because the spirits of my ancestors are telling me to. I'm not sure why, but I will listen to them. Okay, now look here."

Jesús took the little stick and in the middle of the cross he wrote *Yo* (I, me, myself). Next to the intersection of the right arm of the cross and the circle he wrote *Objecto* (object, entity, thing, situation).

He then drew an arrow on the right arm toward the circle and the object point. "When you place your attention on something outside of you, your attention moves in this direction—from you to the object."

He looked up at me to see if I understood and I nodded. Then he drew an arrow on the right arm pointing toward the *me* point. "This is your attention focusing on yourself. But as you can see we now have two arrows. Two points of attention. If you can place your attention on the object and still focus on yourself then you have split your attention in two. This is not a normal state of consciousness for most people.

"During most of a day, attention is placed outward to what we are doing. In some moments we pay attention to our self, especially when we are being careful about what we say or when we are looking in the mirror or when we stub our toe. But we almost always are placing our awareness on one or the other. Either myself or something outside myself. Rarely, or for some people never, do we place our attention on both *at the same time*. This is because it takes a conscious effort to do this and people have never been taught that this is something of value. People are taught to concentrate—concentrate on this, concentrate on that, concentrate on yourself—but not to concentrate on two things at once. If people were taught from childhood to pay attention to themselves while at the same time paying attention to what is around them we would live in a different world."

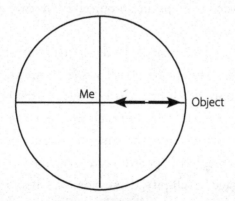

Two points of attention

"So this is different from what we call multitasking?"

Jesús looked at me quizzically. He either didn't understand or I didn't use the proper words in Spanish. So I added, "We call multitasking doing various things at the same time. Like many people drive their car, talk on their cell phone, read a map, and eat a bagel all at the same time. Or maybe I'm typing on my computer while also thinking about a difficult situation with my partner. Isn't our attention split most of the time?"

Chuckling, Jesús replied, "The attention of the object can be used in a multitude of ways. But I am betting that the person driving that car is not paying attention to their essence, to their true being, while they are doing all those other things. That takes a special effort of concentration. And if they were to do that, I also bet that they would immediately stop talking and eating and pay closer attention to their driving. Or maybe they would give up driving altogether. In your other example, thinking about a situation, even one that has to do with yourself, is not the same as paying attention to your inner self. You are placing attention on the details of the situation.

"This *multitasking* you speak of is a learned performance of dealing with life situations. When I make my fire I can easily light a flame, add kindling, blow on it, watch the flames, smell the smoke, and feel the heat all at the same time without ever once placing conscious attention on myself. Placing attention on the object or even objects of what we are doing, and placing attention on ourselves are two completely different states of attention.

"One of the great benefits to the splitting of attention is that when we pay attention to our inner self while we are engaged in something else, we not only touch our true self but the truth about what we are doing. If we are consciously in touch with our true self, the pure spark of God, our essence, and at the same time we see what we are doing, we wouldn't do thoughtless, pointless, mechanical, or cruel things. We also wouldn't engage in self-pity, depression, or self-absorption. Your 'situation' with your partner probably wouldn't have even happened if you were consciously paying attention to yourself and the situation when it was happening.

"This is the hardest truth for people who have lost touch with their essence. It is extremely difficult, almost impossible, for people who have lived their whole lives developing the ego and personality at the expense of the essence to divide their attention and keep it there for any period of time. This is because when attention is placed on the essence at the same time as what we are doing, most people are immediately appalled. The circumstances of how most people live is so extremely out of tune with their essence that it is not even believable. Or even if it is believable it seems too complicated to fix. It is much easier to ignore and just keep going even when to keep going is to keep suffering or leading immature lives. So the answer to your question is that the multitasking you describe is simply one form of attention, the attention that is placed outside of our essence. What I am suggesting is something completely different."

"I'm not clear on what that is?"

"Yes, I realize it's not easy. Until we get to touch our true essence it is difficult. After that it's quite natural. So there are many things we can do to get at the essence, the biggest one is removing the false aspects of the ego, but for now let's concentrate on the points of attention. Placing the attention on yourself will begin with looking internally at your feelings, state of health—physically or mentally, that you are seated in a chair or walking down steps. However, once you have experienced enough times doing this while also paying attention to the object—that which is outside yourself—you will come to a point where the exercise becomes completely different because you will begin to touch your essence.

"For many people this will feel somewhat familiar because they have felt it before. Like I said before, we knew our essence when we were children. We could connect it to being in a new place, around new people, while we were traveling somewhere. This was before we thought we knew all the answers, and our essence wasn't yet overshadowed by our ego and personality. The essence is also sometimes touched in adolescent and adult life when in highly emotional states, or dangerous circumstances, or near-death experiences. In these cases, the controlling parts of the ego and personality break down and we touch the essence.

"So what we require here is to begin with doing something to focus on ourselves at the same time we focus outside ourselves. This in itself is not normal for intellectual people. So the more it is done, the more natural it becomes, and then we begin to feel it in a different way. Instead of just physically or mentally, attention of the essence shines through. But I have news for you. It is incredibly difficult to divide the human attention in two. It is actually easier to divide it into three, four, or best of all, five!"

"That doesn't seem to make much sense."

"Yes, I know! Isn't it wonderful! I love things like that! And this I cannot explain fully to you because I really don't know why it is. But the reality is that it is true. We have an impossible time splitting our attention in two. But dividing attention into three, even though still difficult at first, is much more accessible and beneficial."

"I'm still not getting it."

"Let's use another drawing, maybe it will make it clearer. We will come back to the first drawing sometime later."

He picked up the stick once more and said, "If I put three points anywhere down here, except in a straight line, we will make a triangle right? A triangle has three points."

Jesús made three points in the dirt and connected the points with lines to form the shape of a triangle. "We already said that two points of the attention are me and an object or situation. What do you think the third one is?"

"I'm not sure."

"What else are we involuntarily paying attention to even if we are blind or deaf or both?"

"Where we are?"

"Precisely! The place we are. Where are we? In the office, in the car, in the woods, in the ocean?"

With the stick he labeled the three points—me, object, place. "For whatever reason, our conscious attention doesn't like to travel just in a single line. If we try to put the three points of attention on a single straight line it doesn't work. If we give them each their own line but keep them attached it works perfectly. It's like the points of attention need their own view of each other. It's a spatial thing. By adding the third point it gives the other two points somewhere else to look.

"So this is the exercise I invite you to do. From now on, focus on these three points of attention. Number one—the *me*. Do not forget yourself. Always watch yourself. Pay attention at all times to your words, actions, gestures, habits, even your thoughts and emotions. Number two—the *object*. Be thoroughly attentive to objects, entities, situations, anything outside of you that you can interpret with your senses. Number three—the *place*. Observe at all times where you are and be cognizant of why you are there.

"It is most important to remember *not* to become infatuated with one point of attention. Whether it is yourself, an object, or a place, no matter how interesting, beautiful, horrible, entrancing, or atrocious something is, don't focus one point of attention to such an extent that the others are left out. If you do that you will miss the whole point. When attending to the three points at once becomes natural during your daily life, the challenge is then to keep that attention during

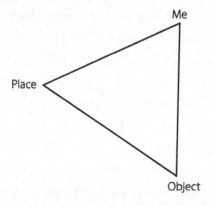

Three points of attention

special circumstances. Once you can keep attentive to all three points even during the stressful or extreme moments of your life you will be ready to proceed to integrating all five points."

"What are the other two points, Jesús?"

"Well, I could tell you. But that would only distract you because once you know of them you will have no choice but to try them. It is best to be proficient at these three first. This is the main task. Once you are proficient at holding these three points of attention at the same time, adding the other two should be simple in comparison because your attention has gotten continually exercised. Your conscious attention will be in great shape!"

Jesús went on to tell me that now that he had explained the three points of attention to me there was no way I wouldn't immediately try them and that I was probably already trying as we spoke. He was right. So he told me to stop because if I really wanted to properly jolt my consciousness and therefore make it more efficient to proceed in the practice, I should introduce my consciousness to this technique in a novel way. Since this is not a normal technique it should initially be employed in a way that is not a normal way.

What he suggested for me to do was focus on the three points of attention while crawling on my hands and knees on the rocky, arid, dusty, scrub-filled ground of the mesa above Teakata. He figured about a kilometer or so would be a good start. Initially I thought his idea was completely crazy. Simply walking with two feet wasn't easy in this terrain, let alone crawling on my hands and knees.

"Right now!" he shouted and pointed a finger at me. "Right now, without crawling, place your attention on me and on the other two points. Focus on yourself, me, and the place where you are. All at the same time."

Jesús was quiet for a few minutes while I did this. "Do you know what a remarkable opportunity this is for you? To learn about this powerful way to handle consciousness right here in one of the most extraordinary places in the world. This is a place of pure magic. It is the center of the Huichol universe."

With that, he stood up and smiled at me while adjusting his morals. His words put me in a different state of mind. He was right. If I was going to wholeheartedly experience this technique of attention, this was a perfect place. It would challenge me on many levels.

"Wherever you can walk, you can certainly crawl on your hands and knees. This is not a race and you are not in a war zone dodging bullets. You are placing yourself in a position of peace, of learning, of higher conscious attention. As far as the crawling goes, you have already done that before in another Huichol sacred place."

Jesús was right. Some years before, I had my one and only "bad trip" while ingesting peyote in Wirikuta and found myself crawling around in the desert for a whole day until I finally "died." I describe this life-changing incident in my book *Ecoshamanism*.

"And as far as using your attention and consciousness in nonordinary ways, you have much experience in that as well."

He was right again; I had more than twenty years of intense experiences working with shamans and medicine people from many different tribes around the globe.

"So for you, the hardest part will be not falling into the trap we spoke of before. As long as you go into this with the spirit of learning something new then you will. If you fall into the trap of thinking you already know, then you will gain nothing."

I understood what Jesús was saying. But I actually wasn't even thinking about it that way. His three points of attention exercise was a new concept to me. And I had only crawled around in the desert once before and it certainly wasn't intentional on my part. To me, this was going to be a new experience and I was going into it in that mindset. The one rational thought I did have was that I was wearing long pants and had a pair of lightweight gloves with me, and I was very happy about that!

"You see that hill over there? I will meet you there whenever you get there. I don't have to tell you to be careful, especially for snakes. You will be traveling quieter, with less vibration than when walking. Remember to place attention on all three points, don't get trapped in just one. Focus on yourself, the various things on the ground in front of you, and the amazing place you are in. Any questions?"

"Just one. If I'm focusing on myself, on what I'm doing, and I'm focusing on the ground while I'm doing it, isn't that like doing the same thing? And if I'm focusing on the ground, isn't that the same as focusing on the place?"

"I'm really glad you asked that question," he said with a laugh. "It shows me you don't have a clue as to what you're talking about! This *will* be a new experience for you. The answer is no. This is exactly what you hopefully will soon find out. Okay. Place attention on yourself *inside*— feel your body and notice your feelings and emotions. Attention of the objects—this will be an awesome experience. Notice all the different plants, rocks, colors, sounds, tastes, smells, everything that is *outside* your body and your head. This *place*—keep cognizant of where you are in the *bigger picture* than just the ground you are crawling on. You are in the middle of a vast and magical place. These three states of attention are completely different to each other although you will try to experience them all at the same time. Remember the symbol of the triangle. These are three points of attention that occupy different places in the space of your consciousness."

The talking was over as Jesús took the things I was carrying and turned and walked quickly away in the direction of the hill he had pointed out to me. I got down on my knees as if praying and as I began to crawl forward on my hands and knees, I wondered if Jesús had known I would feel this way. The action of crawling, at least in the very beginning, really felt like supplication or a petition to a higher power to show me the way. The very act of crawling immediately broke down any feelings of human superiority that I was carrying. I became just one more creature of the desert, and a weak and vulnerable one at that.

Maybe because of the fact that I had so much to concentrate on, or maybe due to the fact that I didn't have to interact with any other people, or maybe it was the magic of the place, or all three, in any case it didn't take me long to perceive all three attentions at once. In retrospect the chief quality I experienced in that state was inner silence. My inner voice that is almost always talking (or singing) just shut up. Paying attention to myself wasn't through words in my mind anymore. It was just some sort of pure knowing and feeling. The tactile sense of feeling everything on the ground with my hands and knees; the visual shapes and colors of rocks, earth, plants, twigs, insects; the taste of dust and sweat; and the sounds of my movement as I touched and crunched along, together with the sounds of the movement of birds in the bushes simply all came as pure perception through my senses with no filters or biases or analysis. The attention of place was most significant as I noticed the fleeting shadows of many little birds crossing to and fro in front of me. A few times I stopped and rose to a kneeling position to view the sky and look ahead to where I was headed. Surprisingly this didn't break my focus on the three attentions, it merely gave me a different sort of angle of perception.

Finally reaching an area close to the hill, I stopped to look ahead and saw Jesús. I crawled the last twenty yards to him. But for whatever reason, seeing him broke my concentration and the final part of my crawl was much different. All kinds of thoughts began running through my head and it became more difficult to crawl. Suddenly the terrain seemed much more demanding and challenging, like it didn't want to let me through. My thoughts were back and they took charge of my attention. When I reached Jesús I finally realized what had happened and I remember thinking that I much preferred the way I felt when I was in tune with all three points of attention and not just the thoughts in my head.

Jesús patted me on the shoulder in a congratulatory way and gave me back my things as I stood up and stretched.

"I could clearly see how well you were doing until you saw me," he said. "Before that you were living the essence. Seeing me put your ego and personality back in charge. In the beginning it is not easy to hold the attention required to live in the essence. But the more you practice, the more natural it will feel. You are now invited to try in all circumstances. When we are together, I will try and help you—especially in those moments when it's most important to be there. This was a very good beginning. As I had hoped, your mind went silent and you connected with your essence for over two hours straight. The more you do it, the less that time or duration will matter. But this was a good first-time experience. Your determination and resolve combined with the place to produce a real result."

As we began to climb down the ravine to Teakata, I asked Jesús to explain the practical purpose of what I had just done. He sort of shook his head and snickered. "What you just did was to focus your attention on the three points and that led you to live for a short period with your essence in charge, instead of your ego and personality. As we talked about before, you have felt your essence and split your attention many times before, probably more than most people. But on most of those occasions you were in some sort of stressful, dangerous, or extremely special situation. There wasn't really anything special this time, except that you initially felt the iyari of the ancestors as we got close to Teakata. The main thing is that you used this new and novel technique that took a great deal of effort but that was accomplished peacefully and with little stress to access your essence. You did it *intentionally.*

"The experience you just had will only be truly practical if you can transfer it to other life situations. For example, when talking to people, working, writing, and so on. If you can focus on your three points of attention during your ordinary life, you will see extraordinary results with regard to your quality of life. It is almost impossible to be living in your true essence and still have unhealthy feelings of anger, depression, arrogance, jealousy, or selfishness. Your essence wants you to discover and live with your true talents and in states of happiness, kindness, cooperation, unity, and wonder. Also, once you have become proficient in living with the attention of the three points, you will then be able to raise your level to five points, which is a most magnificent and mature state of conscious living. People who live solely within their ego and personality cannot possibly comprehend this state of being."

Our visit to Teakata was very much a blur to me as I look back on it. It could have been the powerful energy of the ancestors, or the radical shift in consciousness I just experienced, or remnants in my brain of all the peyote I had ingested in the days before, but for whatever reason I really only remember bits and pieces of it. Maybe that is what the ancestors wanted because even after being in the area of Teakata twice, I don't believe I could find the place on my own. Or if I could, it would take extreme effort and probably a very long time. In any case I would never think about visiting Teakata without being invited.

From what I remember, we first visited a couple of the little shrines in the ravine; then we collected some water from a cave spring that I had not been to before and that was packed full of offerings of jicaras and arrows. Jesús made a big deal out of making sure I kept my little bottle of the sacred water safe on my travels and never drank it. We finally made it to the small kalliway that I had visited once before. The small size of this kalliway, maybe a quarter of the size of those in the ceremonial centers, made it feel more like a large rirriki than a kalliway.

On both occasions, this kalliway did not have a roof, but it was situated under a large cliff. I was told previously that this was the site of the very first kalliway and near to the sacred caves of both Tatewari and Maxakwaxi. I sort of remember visiting one of those caves but I was in such an altered state, I can't write about the experience. What I do remember is that at various places Jesús did his typical marakáme stuff—chanting, waving around his muvieri, crying, and sprinkling deer blood and water on offerings and rocks.

My next full and linear memory was climbing out of the gorge. On our way back to Tuapurie, I asked Jesús about the altered state I had experienced in Teakata. I was feeling very confused because when experiencing the three points of attention and right afterward, my whole being felt so alive and aware. But our time in Teakata seemed all fuzzy and not at all like the peak experience of the three attentions.

"You simply used up your available energy with the exercise of the three attentions," he said. "It takes great effort for modern man to make that breakthrough. It has been referred to as the little death because the dominating ego and personality are switched off. Most men will never even experience it." Jesús stopped on the trail and turned to face me. Standing up straight and tall and in a mock serious voice that resembled a pompous college professor he said, "I think Sir Isaac Newton described it best in the sixteen hundreds: 'For every action there is an equal and opposite reaction.'

"Your attention was pulled so far away from where it normally resides that when released from that far-off place it snapped back and past its usual place where it has come back to now—kind of like the band of a slingshot."

Even though I was feeling quite drained, I somehow knew exactly what he was talking about and it actually made sense to me. Jesús seemed delighted and we returned to our walking without talking.

A couple days later, I returned home to the United States and the only contact I had with the Huichol for more than a year was a few e-mails to and from my friend Casimiro. He and his wife had illustrated my children's book with exceptional Huichol yarn drawings and lived in my house for a few months about two years earlier. Casimiro knows how to send e-mail when he is not in the mountains and has access. So, whenever he travels to sell artwork, he usually contacts me to say hi.

Then one day I received an e-mail from someone with a Huichol name that I didn't recognize. I excitedly opened it and it was from Jesús! He said that he needed to go to Wirikuta and was wondering if I wanted to take him. Maria and two jicareros would also be going, which would make our number five. But surprisingly he also said that if I could come, we would all go to Cerro Gordo first because he wanted me to know the place and complete my five directions and also that Maria had business of her own in Hauxamanaka, the sacred place of the North.

Luckily for me, that time of year was slow for my business and I was able to get away. So two weeks later I found myself crossing the border at Douglas, Arizona, and on my way to Durango where the Huichol agreed to meet me.

Exceptional Ancestor

I met the Huichol near the bus station in Durango. Maria hugged me and introduced me to the jicareros.* One of them, Rafael, I knew slightly from my visits to the Sierra. He was probably in his early thirties, thin but wiry, and very animated for a Huichol. You could just tell that he loved to travel and explore. He was very confident and gave off the feeling that he was a guy you'd like to have around in a crisis or even an altercation. The other jicarero, Marcelino, was a little heavier and about the same age. He came across as sort of a joker but he also appeared to be a tough hombre, like Rafael. With these two guys I would feel safe traveling in Mexico. Jesús was anxious to leave and we all piled in my truck and headed south into the mountains.

On the way, the reasons for this trip were explained to me. "Like I told you, James," Jesús began, "you and Maria have an appointment with the ancestors in Hauxamanaka and I need to go to Wirikuta. I'm going to the peyote fields and I have brought these two jicareros because I want to see what is happening with the hikuri. I have had very disturbing visions. The first thing we need to do is visit with the O'dam because for our work on this trip we need to hunt a deer and they are the custodians of this land."

---

*For the sake of the flow of the narrative, when I speak about the three Huichol other than Jesús I will simply use the word *jicareros*.

"We are close to the place the O'dam call *Maize Gordo* [Plump Corn]," Jesús said excitedly after about two hours of driving in an extremely rural part of Mexico that seemed almost completely empty of people. "Here lives the headman called Pancho Villa."

The other Huichol all laughed at this so Jesús added, "I don't know if that is his real name or not. But that's what all the people call him. He is a big and tough hombre just like the general Pancho Villa from Durango was. But you know it does not matter if that is not his real name because the real name of the famous general Pancho Villa was actually José!"

The Huichol were rolling with laughter and in a supremely good mood. I parked the vehicle, noticing once again how remote a mountainous area we were in. We walked a short distance to a small house. Jesús knocked on the door, and a large man with an even larger mustache came to the door with a lantern. He looked at all of us and then told us to wait. A few minutes later, he came out and shook hands with all of us and led us down a trail around and in back of his house. I was extremely surprised to see a structure almost identical to a Huichol kalliway. The only apparent difference was the lack of rirrikis to the East of the temple.

We entered the O'dam temple and Pancho invited the Huichol to light a fire in the central fire pit. Within minutes, the expert fire makers had a blaze going and Jesús and Pancho got down to business while we sat around the fire. They agreed that we would pay 1,000 pesos (around eighty U.S. dollars) to hunt in a prescribed area known to both of the men and that we could kill one deer, but only a male deer. The area was on O'dam land and Pancho gave Jesús a sort of receipt with an official seal on it, after I gave him the thousand pesos. Jesús explained that we were there primarily for the blood and mask of the deer including the antlers and that we would happily share the meat with the O'dam. This went over quite well with Pancho, and he invited us to stay the night in or around the kalliway. Jesús thanked him and declared confidently that we would be back with a male deer at night the day after tomorrow. Pancho didn't flinch at the self-assuredness of the Huichol mara-káme but rather stated that he would gladly gather some of his people to meet us here when we returned in two nights with the deer.

After gathering our things for the night and some more firewood, I got a chance to ask Jesús about the O'dam. The inside of the O'dam kalliway was not adorned like those of the Huichol but the shape and the feeling of the place was close to identical. Jesús said that the Huichol and the *Tepehuan,* known as the O'dam in their southernmost region closest to the Huichol, had a long history together—so much so that their languages are quite similar. Jesús explained that Huichol folklore tells us that it was Maxakwaxi himself that united the Tepehuanes and the Coras and Huichol many ages ago. But after Maxakwaxi died and became an ancestor god the relationship between the tribes deteriorated and they were enemies for a long time.

"Throughout the ages we have been both friends and enemies. Right now in this time we are friends again and the O'dam realize that although the Mexican government says that this is their land, no one really owns the earth. O'dam, like Pancho, understand that our people have hunted here for many ages and that this area is sacred to us even though we don't live here, just like our sacred sites of Wirikuta, Xapawiyeme, and Haramara. At one time, some of the O'dam even lived where we do now. We have kept back the Mexicans better than they have, and we have kept our traditions better too. But in their hearts the O'dam are closer to the Huichol, probably more than anyone else."

I asked Jesús why we needed to pay Pancho to hunt a deer. He explained that it was really just a formality, a gesture of respect. In the mind of the Huichol, including Jesús, they did not need anyone's permission to visit their ancestral sacred sites and to hunt deer or peyote, no matter who claimed to own the land. He said that they had an agreement with the O'dam about visiting this sacred area of Hauxamanaka. If we did not have any money, we could still do what we came here for. But because this time we did have something to offer them, in the spirit of cooperation it was good that we do so. Since there are no more wild deer in the Huichol Sierra, in other parts of the Sierra where the Huichol have to go to hunt deer for their pilgrimages they have to pay the Mexican landowners. The Mexicans usually only agree if they know the marakáme and have had relations with him before. And of course they have to pay or trade. It can be a very difficult and political situation. With the O'dam, the money we gave them was more like a gift than a requirement.

Since we were traveling to a major sacred site on more or less a pilgrimage, I knew that the Huichol would probably not eat or sleep. That was their custom during these situations. So I wrapped myself in my blanket and spent the night lightly snoozing and partly dreaming to the dancing light of the fire and the guttural speech of the Huichol as they chatted quietly throughout the night.

Before dawn, the fire was put out and we were on our way again. We again drove on dirt roads that were hardly even there. After maybe forty-five minutes we stopped at a gorgeous area that, if I had been walking all this way, I would have thought was a mirage. In reality what it turned out to be was a natural spring that formed a small lagoon from which began a stream flowing out into the land. This area was lush with vegetation and trees and you could really feel the life energy emanating from it. On the opposite side of the lagoon, I could make out what looked like a place full of colorful Huichol offerings. Once we all grabbed our morals, we walked over there.

Jesús explained that this was a sacred spot of Great-Grandfather Deer Tail. Here we would anoint ourselves with eternal water and leave our offerings for a successful hunt. He said that Maxakwaxi was there watching us from the bushes and we had to be respectful and leave him nice gifts to feed his soul.

The procedure for leaving offerings was similar to other sacred springs I had been to with the Huichol. Together the pilgrims give prayers with their rhythmic speech and offer gourds with beaded figures and prayer arrows and candles and chocolates and small yarn drawings that the marakáme blesses with his muvieris and chants.

Once the offerings were given and consecrated, we one by one followed Maria's lead and went into the water to be blessed and cleansed. It was a most sublime experience, and after getting out I felt much cleaner than simply in a physical sense. Although I did need a bath, what I felt more was a deep connection between the water of my body and the water of the lagoon. Knowing that over half of the makeup of my physical body is water, I was not surprised to feel such a connection. However, this sacred place of the Huichol somehow flowed into me the awareness of how much I actually am water to a whole new level, and I silently understood even better why the Huichol make pilgrimages to honor and visit such places.

After our baptism in the lagoon, we hiked for a while toward what appeared to be a rising slope. The trees became taller and thicker and soon afterward we were definitely walking up hill. Rock boulders and small hills of rock began appearing and suddenly a high rock wall appeared off to our right. We headed toward the wall, and I began to make out a cave-like overhang with more Huichol offerings inside. Above the overhang were more offerings that people had placed way up there. It looked like an extremely dangerous place to climb up in order to leave offerings.

Jesús pointed up to the place and told me that at one time there was a really big kieri plant growing there. I knew about the dangerously psychoactive kieri, usually a species of solandra but sometimes datura as well. He explained that evil sorcerers prayed to the kieri and used it to put hexes on people. They were the ones leaving offerings to the kieri above the cave. However, the kieri itself was not all bad and was a very powerful ancestor. There was a very complex Huichol myth about Peyote-man battling and defeating Kieri-man. Afterward Peyote-man petitioned the gods to make Kieri-man less evil and so they did. Jesús said that we would leave offerings here in the sacred place of the kieri, not because we wanted something but simply out of respect for an ancient and powerful ancestor. He said that there were still kieri plants growing in the area and that our offering was similar to the offering that we gave to Pancho's people. Instead of ignoring them or the kieri, it was much better to respectfully acknowledge them and bring them gifts. This was a sign of reciprocity and respect.

The night before the deer hunt found us back at the sacred lagoon where the Huichol sparked up the grandfather fire in their typical ceremonial manner. I was glad we came back to the lagoon because, first of all, the place of the kieri creeped me out for some reason. I guess it was all the talk about evil sorcerers. Second, even though we had an agreement with the O'dam headman, this was still extremely rural Mexico and I felt much better being in close proximity to my vehicle for many reasons.

Anyway, my informant Maria casually mentioned to me that this was a supremely important night—maybe the most important of our whole trip. She disclosed that it was essential for the marakáme to locate our special deer in the spirit world so that he could successfully complete his offering to us.

"But why would the deer want to die for us?" I questioned. "Doesn't he want to live and be free and do deer things? Aren't they so quiet and aware and fast so that they don't get killed by predators?"

"Of course they are so awake in their mind with their giant ears and nose, and so fast and agile with their strong springy legs, and especially their swishy tail that they rhythmically twitch back and forth like a supernatural radar. That's why we respect them so much! They are purely magical beings, they are our brothers. But even more than that—some of them are our ancestors. Our deer will come to us because he wants to be with his people again. But we have to convince him that we are who we say we are. That he is not being tricked. Our job tonight is to prove to him that we are his descendants and that he would choose very well to come join us because we still keep the ancient traditions and honor the sacred sites and the ancestors. Not only do we need to prove we are worthy of his sacrifice—many Huichol that follow the tradition are worthy—we need to show him we are special, that we will be exceptional companions for him. And in return he will allow us the use of his iyari, by means of his sacred blood. It's like a partnership. But just like any partnership you have to trust your partners. This deer that we want to join us has already proved his commitment to our traditions because he is already here living in this sacred place. It is us who need to prove to him that someday we will follow in his footsteps."

"So you're saying that this deer was a Huichol?"

"Of course! I thought you knew all this," she replied while shaking her head.

When I explained that I was pretty sure I didn't know what she was talking about, she continued to explain, "All of the main sacred places we go to on our pilgrimages have multiple meanings for us. More precisely there are multiple manifestations of our ancestors living there. This area, our sacred place in the North, is just like that. There are many things—many places, many animals, many plants, many folktales, many histories, many ancestors—that are here that are sacred and special to us. Among other things, this is a place of the dead come back to life.

"Exceptional Huichol who live their lives according to our ancestors and keep our traditions alive in the face of constant threats are rewarded when they die. We don't have time right now for me to try and explain all this to you. It is a big subject. But in this case let's just say that this deer we are hoping to meet tomorrow is one of our ancestors, probably a talented marakáme or even a kawitéro from the past. This area we call Hauxamanaka is a place where some of our exceptional ancestors choose to be reborn because by doing that they are continuing the sacred loop. They know that exceptional Huichol will come here to ask them to join them. Our part of the loop is to ask appropriately and to prove ourselves in the hunt. Their part of the loop is to offer to "play," and if we are exceptional enough to catch them, then they will bless us and everything we touch with their blood. That way we complete the loop together. We make blessings to the sacred places and our offerings with their iyari, in the physical form of their blood, and they get to travel with us and be part of the ceremonies and pilgrimages once again."

Maria took her leave to get her things ready for the night, and I did the same while pondering all that she had just told me. Until that moment, I had no idea that this sacred place of the North was a place of the Huichol dead. Knowing how complex their tradition was, I was certain there was a heck of a lot more that I still didn't know about the subject of the Huichol dead and, more important at the moment, the sacred area I was standing in.

That night was the first time I got to hear a future female marakáme sing. She was outstanding as the supporting singer for Jesús. I had only once met a female marakáme. She was appointed to be the wet-season marakáme of the Las Latas temple when the original marakáme, whom I'm told was close to ninety years old, fell ill and died during his third year of that five-year cycle. Unfortunately I did not witness any ceremonies in which she sang. Listening to Maria sing the responses to her grandfather was surreal for me on many levels. First of all, as I said, I had never heard a female cantador before. Sure, in most if not all Huichol ceremonies that I have witnessed or been a part of, many if not all of the group of participants chant back to the marakáme at some point. But they are not chant-singing in the same way as the marakáme and his assistants. The other people participating sort of mumble, for lack of a better description, in a much more subdued manner. It is not really their job, or task, to sing perfect responses back to the marakáme but rather to lend general support and energy to the singers.

Being in a similar trance state as the marakáme and chanting back to him is the task of the assistants who are typically either marakámes themselves or future marakámes. What impressed me most about Maria is that in the same way I have seen very soft-spoken marakámes completely transform their voice and personality while chanting, so did Maria. This very unassuming and humble young woman sang with such intensity and concentration and connection that it gave me goose bumps and I had to make a conscious effort to close my mouth, which was gaping open as I stared at her. I could immediately tell why Jesús was supporting her. This woman was exceptional to say the least and I was sure would someday be a potent marakáme.

Aside from the transformation in her attitude, the second thing about Maria that struck me was her voice. Even though the chant-singing of Huichol marakámes in general is similar, each marakáme has a unique style or delivery. Maria's style was so expressive and eloquent that she basically put me into a trance listening to her. She had the guttural and deep vocalizations of the male marakáme but her high notes were much sweeter and cleaner than I had ever heard before.

If all that wasn't enough, I couldn't help but be completely impressed by her stamina. Of course her job wasn't nearly as difficult or taxing as her grandfather's. Jesús was the main singer and she was simply responding to him in not so many words. But to stay focused and sing so exceptionally all night long was something amazing to behold. I felt extremely privileged to witness such an outstanding performance. If the spirit of the deer wanted a show of proof that these were worthy Huichol, I was sure he was getting what he came for.

Somewhere around halfway through the night of Jesús and Maria singing, Rafael whispered to me to pay close attention. He said that Jesús was going to start looking for the deer in the spirit world. I watched intently as Maria handed him a woven piece of cloth maybe four inches square. Rafael said that Maria had woven the spirit of the deer into the patterns of that piece of cloth and that Jesús was going to sing with it to find the deer it belonged to.

I looked at him quizzically and he explained, "She has been learning how to find deer in her dreams and she found this ancestor over a year ago. After she found him, she has been feeding him the favorite things he likes to eat, like his favorite grasses, apples, and especially what he can't find here, like chocolate and salt. She has been waiting a long time to meet him in person.

"So how will she find out where he is?"

"That is the job of the marakáme. Our women don't physically hunt for the deer. They make offerings to the deer before and after the hunt but we men have to catch them. The marakáme must use his powers of vision to see where this deer of Maria's likes to go so that we can catch him. That is part of our test as a group. Maria has woven a small part of his soul into her fabric with her loom. At home she is also learning to be a master weaver. She gave the soul part to Jesús in order for him to find it. When he finds the deer, he will weave webs along the trails with a special muvieri so that the deer will come to where we want him. Then we—Rafael, you, and me—will make the actual trap. It's teamwork."

And so it was that the marakáme held that piece of cloth along with his muvieris for the rest of the night's singing. I can't claim to have experienced anything like what Jesús and Maria must have but it was an amazing performance that I will never forget.

Somehow during the night while chanting with the Grandfather Fire, Jesús was told where the deer that was to offer himself to us would be. This skill, along with bringing rain when needed, is a sure sign of a mature marakáme who can be likened to a Christian saint who can perform miracles. In the case of a marakáme like Jesús, he doesn't make a miracle happen but instead *allows* the miracle to happen through the participation of the ancestors. In the predawn light, Jesús explained to us that *Bisabuelo Cola del Ciervo* (Great-Grandfather Deer Tail) showed him a thick area of scrub trees where four deer trails came together. In the center we should put our snare.

Quickly we packed up our things and followed Jesús, except for Maria. When I asked about that, I was told again that women do not participate in the actual hunt. Almost immediately we were on a barely perceptible deer trail in thick brush. Although easy for the deer, it was very difficult for us to get through it without rubbing and scratching on the bushes and branches. The murky trail was noticeable on the ground but the brush above it was thick and we basically needed to squat way down or sometimes even crawl to get through it. When I was young and used to deer hunt a lot growing up in Pennsylvania, I watched deer, mostly bucks, crawl through the brush on many occasions.

The going was slow but within about half an hour we stopped, and Jesús silently pointed to the ground and to the four cardinal directions. In each direction was a vague deer trail, and we were standing in the center of the intersection.

Without talking, the jicareros set their snare while I tried my best to help them. Basically the snare was comprised of a horizontal branch that was hung with cordage about the height of the deer. To this was hung a noose attached to a wooden trigger (a stick notched into the shape of the number 7) that was attached with cordage to a sturdy but thin tree that they bent down onto the horizontal branch. When the deer hit the branch the trigger would snap, the noose would slip around the deer's neck, and the thin tree would bend back into position capturing the deer. This set up would not kill the deer but merely catch him until the hunters came.

With the snare set at the appointed place we quietly left the area the same way we came in. During the morning hours, I helped the Huichol make a really beautiful stretcher, or litter, to carry the deer away on. Maria was the leader and supervisor of this task. It was constructed of branches and sticks for the frame with reeds and grass and flowers as the bed. Once the stretcher was ready, we went part of the way back to the snare to wait and spent the remainder of the day sitting quietly in the thick brush dozing dreamily and sharpening knives. It was beginning to get quite dark when Rafael suddenly stood up and pointed toward the snare. We all stood and listened intently and after a few moments I distinctly heard the bleat of a deer in the distance.

Carefully and quietly we made our way to the snare and indeed there was a buck caught in the jicareros trap. Since I grew up with deer that made their home surrounded by corn and alfalfa fields, apple orchards and acorn-laden oak forests, I thought this deer looked very small for its age (I'm guessing three or four years old), since there was only wild forage for it to eat. But I sensed the Huichol were quietly ecstatic at their catch and quickly and efficiently had the buck hanging upside down with its feet tied.

The next thing that happened came as a complete surprise to me; Maria walked reverently up to the deer, kissed its nose while stroking the top of his head, said a few words I didn't hear, and then placed the nose and mouth of the deer inside her mouth. Maria took a few deep breaths and then gently released the deer and backed away. These were the final breaths of the deer. Jesús quickly prayed over the animal and when finished, Marcelino expertly slit its throat. The jicareros were ready with containers and collected all the deer's blood. I never dreamed that a captured deer could be so peaceful. It didn't thrash around or make any sounds once the Huichol had him. This fact coupled with (in my mind) the truly miraculous manner in which this deer was found and captured is something that still boggles my mind.

The Huichol now did two last things after untying him and laying him on the ground. With extreme care and ridiculously sharp knives, they removed the face of the deer, which they then tied to a board of similar size and reverently wrapped up to take with them. Then they cut open the deer's belly and while gutting it methodically removed what they called the *nierika* of the deer, which looked to me like a piece of the intestines that was shaped like a spiral. The spiral of the inside of the deer was buried where it had died "so the iyari of the deer will come back to this place." The deer was then gently placed on its "grass bed" and Maria sprinkled water onto its tongue and placed pieces of chocolate and corn next to his mouth. This was all done in such a reverential way I had tears in my eyes, as did the Huichol. It truly felt as emotional as a human funeral. At one point Marcelino looked up at me and quietly said something to the effect of, "My dream is to come back as a deer to this place when I die. Maybe one day you will come and take my blood so that I can visit all the sacred places again."

I was intrigued about all the conversations and references to what sounded to me as a type of reincarnation but in that moment it didn't feel appropriate to ask for an explanation. I would try to find out more from Jesús at another time.

Even though it was now dark, the Huichol insisted we take the deer to the O'dam. We took turns carrying the funeral stretcher with the deer to my truck, and a couple hours later we were back at the house of the headman Pancho Villa. He was there with some other tribal members and they seemed very pleased and impressed that we had captured the deer exactly when Jesús said we would. Together the Huichol and O'dam blessed the deer and thanked him inside the O'dam kalliway. Afterward some of the O'dam men began the butchering process and shortly later we were served some pieces of roasted deer meat by the women who had cooked it.

As agreed upon, we left the deer with the O'dam as a gift and also because it wasn't practical to take it with us on our trip to Wirikuta. I felt supremely confident that every part of the deer would be used and treated with equal respect as the Huichol would have done in their part of the Sierra. And I'm sure Jesús felt the same. As we were about to leave, Jesús lingered outside the truck as if waiting for something. A few moments later, Pancho Villa came with something wrapped in a plastic bag and with a respectful bow handed it to Jesús. The two men shook hands and said goodbye. Now the hunt was complete—we had the blood, face, and antlers of the ancestor as part of our group. Jesús took the antlers out of the bag and placed them on the dashboard with the tines pointing ahead. He smiled at me and turning to look at the others it occurred to me that we really had done exceptionally well.

The Pyramid Effect

Personally, at this point I was ready to find a cozy bed and sleep the night through, but the Huichol were all fired up and wanted to press on. With the spirit of an exceptional ancestor now with us, they were energized to fulfill their visit to Hauxamanaka and then travel onward to Wirikuta. Their enthusiasm was contagious as they blew their bull horns and played their little instruments while rhythmically pounding their feet on the floor of the truck. I was caught up in a whirlwind of Huichol tradition, cosmology, mythology, and the spirits of the ancestors. Trusting Jesús knew where he was going, we headed toward the mountain called Cerro Gordo.

When we arrived where Jesús was headed, he was not too happy and the music abruptly stopped. Apparently things had changed since he was there last. He explained that there was a new road leading up into the mountain. We were stopped at an intersection of two deeply rutted dirt roads with a large parking area on one side and what looked like a whole acre of cut logs on the other. The cleared parking area had a number of logging trucks parked with a few men lingering around them doing maintenance. In the back part of the parking area there seemed to be a row of small cabins, which was probably housing for the lumbermen.

I guess the Huichol were used to hiking up the mountain from close to where we now were, but now there was a road going farther up the mountain. It was agreed to continue and see where the road would take us. It seemed pretty clear the logging trucks would not be running again until morning. Just as we were about to start up, a man knocked on my window. He introduced himself as the *jefe* (boss) and asked what we were doing there. He was definitely Mexican and not O'dam. I told him we were going to the top of the mountain, and as he peered inside the truck and saw the Huichol, he snickered and said that he was told by the O'dam that some Indians in bright costumes might come along.

He told us that they were not logging near to the sacred site that the O'dam told them about and that we were free to use their road if we wanted to. It would take us partway. He reached into his jacket and produced a pad of papers from which he pulled off the top sheet and handed it to me. It showed the logo of the logging company with a number printed underneath. The jefe instructed me to place it on the dashboard and that way his men would know that we had spoken with him if they came upon my truck. I was surprised he had given us permission without first securing a bribe, which was not only typical but even expected in Mexico. But after handing me the paper he just stood there, so I took that as a sign and offered him a fifty-peso bill, which he readily took.

We left the jefe and began our journey upward but the feeling inside the truck had become tense. I could only relate to what the Huichol must have been feeling by remembering when I had gone back to visit special places in nature I had known while growing up. Twenty years later, they were mostly erased and replaced with subdivisions. My heart felt broken and I found it extremely sad that the people living in those homes had no idea of the forest, ponds, and wildlife that used to be there. For the Huichol, I'm sure this feeling was even more amplified by knowing that countless generations of Huichol had come to this sacred place before the invention of modern logging equipment. In that moment, our trip took on an even more urgent mood as we drove past vast areas of clear-cut forest. The ancient customs of reciprocity and the modern reality of greed had hit us head on.

Thankfully the logging road only extended a few miles in the direction we wanted to go and I parked in an out-of-the-way place mostly hidden from the road. Near to the end of the road was a large open structure with a roof that resembled a giant carport. Jesús said we would spend the night there and begin our trek up the mountain on foot in morning. I was relieved by this decision—happy to be out of the truck and not driving, and also for a rest before our hike. I was also looking forward to the chance to speak to Jesús about personal stuff, as we really hadn't had the chance yet on this whirlwind trip.

I got my opportunity a little while later as we all settled in around the fire for the night. Surprisingly Maria began the conversation by asking me if I had been practicing the technique of the three attentions.

"You know about that?" I asked.

"Well, sure," she replied confidently. "I was a student of Jesús before you came along," she added playfully.

"So you practice the three attentions too?"

"I did a few years ago. It came very naturally to me since I am Huichol and a woman. Huichol learn these kinds of thing fast because we don't have TVs and computers and cars and all that other stuff that distracts one's attention. And women generally learn much quicker than men because we have a womb that directly connects us to the forces of creation and the cycles of the world. This makes us more adaptable. Men are very rigid and stubborn."

"Watch your mouth, little girl," Rafael lightheartedly chimed in. But he didn't disagree with her. Jesús sat silently but listening intently. By the look on his face and his posture while Maria spoke, I could tell he was very proud of her.

Maria continued, "I began focusing on the three attentions just like you and soon after it just became natural for me, so Jesús taught me about the other two. Now I use the five attentions almost all the time without even really thinking about it. Learning this has helped my weaving, my dreaming, and my singing."

"What about *your* practice?" Jesús inquired bluntly.

I had been desiring to speak to him about this subject for many months, but now that the time came I was drawing a blank. Without thinking, I looked to the fire and immediately placed myself into the awareness of my three attentions. Somehow I could feel that the Huichol knew about my shift in awareness and quietly Maria whispered to me, "Muy bien [very good]."

With my attention simultaneously placed on myself, the conversation, and our setting, I began to recount my successes and failures with the practice to my friends. All in all I had been very successful in cultivating the awareness of the three attentions at will. What I lacked was the ability to stay there all the time. I would very naturally simply get sucked into whatever it was I was doing, which placed my attention more squarely on the object, so then I would eventually have to intentionally realize that and try to go back to the attention of three. It is amazing how trained my awareness was to constantly being in only one attention. I could easily expand to three when I intended to, but in the beginning, without even realizing it, I would revert back to one.

Eventually the more I practiced, the easier it became to stay aware of where my attention was going. During the first six months to eight months, I actually set the alarm on my sports watch (which I bought just for this reason) to beep in thirty-minute increments so I could place my attention back to three. Once back there, I would reset the alarm again. It was really cool when finally I began to hear the timer while still aware of my three attentions during the course of my normal day.

The Huichol all laughed quietly as I spoke about my timer. Jesús simply shook his head and I could tell he was dying to interject some comical comment but he held back and allowed me to continue.

The two main things I noticed about raising my awareness to the attention of the three points was that I felt a lot more calm but I also had a lot more energy. I even had people I know and friends of mine comment to me on both points. I was naturally kind of a hyper person who had to make a conscious effort to stay still or keep quiet. And at the end of the day, or even sometimes in the middle of the day, I felt burned out. Both of those qualities had changed markedly for the better when I learned how to be aware of my attention.

Maria and Jesús both seemed pleased at what I had discovered and Maria explained that they were tied together. Habitually focusing on one attention leaves the other aspects of our attention unnourished. Even if we are extremely successful in what we are placing that single attention on, we are still living only partially in our true essence. Without nourishing our full essence, it is normal to feel burned out, thin, grumpy, depressed, and even worse, getting to the point of acting out our anger and frustration. When we are aware of ourselves, our object, and our place all at once we make much sounder decisions about where to place our energy. By placing our energy on activities that not only don't drain us but enhance us, we naturally feel more energized because we actually do have more available energy.

Maria took a muvieri from her takwatsi and drew the symbol of the five directions in the dirt between us. She looked to her grandfather and he nodded his head in agreement.

"Grandfather told me before this trip that if you were ready he wanted me to unveil the two remaining points to you. The two remaining points are below, or underneath, and above, or beyond."

Maria then pointed to the five points on the drawing. The center was me, the right point the object, the left point the place, the bottom point the underneath, and the top point the beyond.

"Now as you can see all the points are connected. You can also imagine that if I were to pull up the center point the curved lines of the

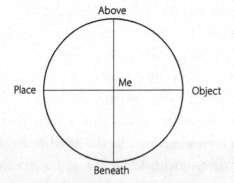

Five points of attention

Four-sided pyramid with point at top

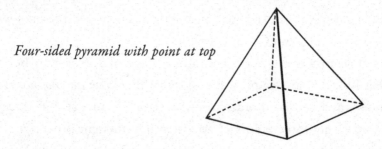

circle would straighten and we would now have a four-sided pyramid with a point at the top.

As soon as Maria said that, I had a vague memory suddenly come clearly into my mind. The memory was about the time Jesús had taken me to Teakata. At some point while visiting the cave shrines, one of them had a small pyramid placed among all the other offerings. The pyramid was about a foot high and seemed to be made of compacted dirt or clay. It was fashioned to have five distinct levels and I remember wondering to myself what it was doing there. It seemed so out of place with all the usual beaded gourd bowls, arrows, candles, and yarn drawings that were typical of Huichol offerings. I had never seen a pyramid of any kind in all my time with the Huichol except on that one occasion. It also occurred to me that I had heard of Huichol visiting the pyramids at Teotihuacán outside Mexico City but I never knew why and I really didn't think to ask.

Somehow reading my thoughts, Maria continued, "The five points of attention and the significance of the number five were well known to the exceptional ancient people who built many of the pyramids throughout Mexico. I'm guessing that you know some of them?"

"Yes," I replied, a little surprised that we were having this conversation. "I have had interesting and sometimes even amazing experiences at the pyramids of Teotihuacán, Uxmal, Palenque, Chichén Itzá, and others."

"Have you ever visited the pyramids in Egypt?" she asked.

"No, not yet. Maybe someday," I replied. "I haven't really had the urge to go there."

"I have not been there either, probably for the same reasons as you, but I have seen photos as I'm sure you have, too. Do you recall any major differences between the great pyramids in Egypt and the ones we have here in Mexico and Central America?"

The answer did not come right to my mind. Normally because of that I would have simply just said something lame like *no, not really* or shook my head *no* in order to just receive the answer. But since I was aware of my three points of attention, my thought process was much clearer and I was able to pull my mind back and quickly survey the situation. Almost immediately images from different places, many that I had been to and some that I had only seen in photos and videos, came to mind and I had the answer.

"The Egyptian pyramids are pointed at the top and they don't have steps. They were not built for people to get to the top."

"Exactly," Maria said with a smile. The Egyptians made their pyramids for different reasons, even though they obviously understood the power of the five points. The exceptional ancient ones over here made their pyramids flat on top. And many times they even had an open chamber on top with a roof. And always they had steps on the outside so you could go up there. That's because that is the center point that connects all the others. The ancients that made the pyramids that you have visited didn't make them just to look at, or as a monument to the dead. Oh, no. They made them to be *used* for focusing attention on the five points. After Grandfather explained to me about the five points of attention, I sold all my weavings—bags, belts, and everything—so I could visit the pyramids of Mexico. Many of the ones you mentioned are my favorites.

"Once you fully comprehend the five points of attention, not just intellectually but with your pure essence, it's simple to understand why the ancient people went through so much work to construct them. To this day, modern scientists living in one attention at a time still can't figure out how most of the pyramids were even built, or even how the ancients got the materials there to build them. With all their fancy machines and big words, modern people who have lost connection to their essence are immature beings trapped in a one-dimensional life. They will never grasp knowledge beyond their ego and personality living in one attention. The ancient people who built the four-sided pyramids with platforms on the top and steps to reach them were living in a totally different reality than most people do now.

"It really is profoundly sad that millions of tourists every year go to pyramids like Chichén Itzá and learn basically nothing about the human faculties of attention. I have seen people at the top of Chichén Itzá and the Pyramid of the Sun at Teotihuacán have a special moment. And I thought about trying to help them hang on to that but what can I do? I am a Huichol woman from the Sierra just visiting places outside our mountains. When they come down from the top after taking their photos they immediately enter back into their normal 'city' awareness and soon forget all about it. Even with all the sleeping tourists, my favorite is still Chichén Itzá. What an inspiring creation that pyramid is— beautiful steps on all four sides leading up to the Center. You can climb up the North and come down the South or climb up like the Father Sun in the East and later come down as the setting sun on the West. When you are standing or sitting at the top you are the fifth point of the four-sided pyramid. You are the center of the universe. That is exceptional!"

I had to agree that what she was saying did ring true and that I had even thought about the five points of the four-sided pyramids before when I had climbed them. It's certainly not difficult, if you are open to it, to experience *something* different in your perception when you are at the top of one of those ancient pyramids, even if you know nothing

Five-pointed pyramid of Chichén Itzá with steps to the top point

about them. Listening to Maria, I wished that I had had knowledge of what she was telling me when I had visited them in the past.

"Don't worry, I'm sure you'll go visit some of them again," Jesús said. "You're way too curious not to!"

"That's right," Maria added. "Maybe I will even go with you. Someday when I get my passport I want to go to Tikal too. But let's not focus on that now. Grandfather Jesús has asked me to explain this to you so I have to try and do an exceptional job. I have just told you about the two remaining points of attention but that doesn't mean you understand them. It should be obvious to you that we recognize the concept of the pyramids and sometimes exceptional Huichol employ that shape in offerings or power objects. But in general, all Huichol prefer to view the universe as well as consciousness in forms that are round and circular. That is why our temples are round and not square. For this discussion let's move on from the pyramid and go back to the circle with five points. In order to understand the points below and beyond we can add this visual aid to our circle.

"You see, for us, we conceive the world as a giant jicara, a great big ceremonial gourd. In the middle of this gourd is where we live—the place of the five directions. Then there is also what is under and what is over. Someone who is very good at drawing could make this diagram in three dimensions and it would look nicer, but I'm sure you get the idea. Right?"

I nodded affirmatively and was truly excited to hear what she was going to say next. I had waited a long time for this!

"Okay. Let's start with the attention of below, or under. This can also be called the *root* attention. But before we go any further, I have to tell

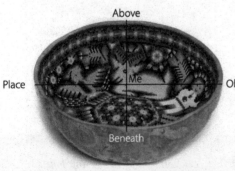

Ceremonial gourd with the five points of attention (gourd bowl beaded by Sylvestre Castro)

you about a truth. This truth is similar to the truth about the first three attentions. The truth is this—the fourth and fifth attentions are a pair that work together just like the first three work together. Nobody knows why it is almost impossible to focus awareness on yourself, the *subject,* and something outside of you, the *object,* at the same time without adding the third point, *place.* You have already confirmed this for yourself and anyone with the proper intent can confirm it as well. In this same respect, it is virtually impossible to add either of the other two points of attention to the first three without adding them both together. Understand?"

"Sure. Okay. You don't go from three to four, you have to go from three to five."

"For that simple but incomprehensible reason I'm going to help you understand the next point of attention, which in this case will be the attention of the underneath, but don't even bother trying to add this point to your other three points until I have explained to you the essence of the fifth point. Just be patient, listen, and try to comprehend without moving your attention from the three points you are currently living. If you do you will just drain your energy and probably not get to experience all five points together. I hope I am making myself clear. Some people who don't listen to this advice never make the union of the five points. They live in the awareness of the three points, which can be a nice life. But that is not the objective. To be exceptional we have to cross the boundary from three to five."

Jesús suddenly broke into the discussion and told me to arrange the fire in a new way as Maria explained to me about the fourth attention. He instructed me to take the arrows (sticks) of the fire that were pointed toward our destination (the top of the Cerro Gordo) and make a teepee or pyramid with them and other new sticks. I could move the pillow log or keep it where it was, it didn't matter.

I immediately figured he was having me do this to distract me from trying to add the fourth point to the first three without the fifth point. In retrospect it was the perfect distraction because, first of all, I love playing with fire, and second the numinous quality of the flames made it easier to be calm and patient as I held my three points of attention in balance.

Maria began her instruction. "The fourth point of attention we will now speak of is that which is seemingly below or underneath our normal states of perception. This includes awareness of the physical world that we do not see during our normal day. The roots of trees that allow them to grow, worms that give life to the soil, seeds that are waiting to sprout, leaves and branches decomposing into the ground, underground rivers, minerals, fossils, magma, crystals, bones, dead people, lost cities, ants and woodchucks and tarantulas, snakes and rabbits and bears in their dens. Sewers, subways, electric and gas lines, tunnels and mines, rats and homeless people, landfills, toxic waste, secret stashes, hidden bunkers, nuclear missiles, basements, oil, and garages. These are a few of the things beneath us every day but we don't normally attend to them. We do not normally place conscious awareness to what is under us. But why not?

"On the other hand there are countless senses, intuitions, and conditions of primal awareness or instinct that we don't normally attend to, either. As an example let's begin with the mother of the fourth attention—intuition. How would you define intuition?"

"Knowing something without knowing how I know it," I replied.

"The eminent psychologist Carl Jung defined it as *perception by way of the subconscious*," Jesús stated very slowly and in a mock tone of a college professor, which made everyone chuckle and lightened the mood.

"Yes!" Maria declared emphatically. "Knowing without knowing how you know, subconscious perceiving, knowing without using logic or reason. Intuition is underneath our normal rational awareness and sits squarely in the point of the fourth attention.

"So how about other examples?" she asked.

"Humor!" exclaimed Marcelino while pointing a finger at Jesús.

"Excellent example," Maria replied happily. "What makes something funny? Why do some people laugh at something and other people don't? Maybe they just don't get it. Or maybe they do get it but they don't consider it funny. Whatever the case, the essence of what makes something funny is hidden underneath."

"Fear," Rafael added in a mock scary voice.

"Exactly," Maria agreed. "How do we know to be afraid of something? Maybe we learned that certain things or situations are dangerous. But the core essence of fear lies underneath reason. Like the pure instinct of survival, to fight or run with no time to think about it."

"Sexual attraction," Jesús added, trying to sound sexy but failing miserably.

"Okay, Grandpa, that's a good one," Maria replied sarcastically. "Attraction is as mysterious as intuition or anything else involving the mind of the fourth attention. We don't know why we are attracted to certain people or food or trees or animals, we just are. Attraction lies underneath reason.

"Are you getting the theme here, James?" Maria asked with more seriousness.

"Yes. But wouldn't I be aware of these things while I'm being attentive of myself or attentive to the object or place?"

"Good question. But remember that everything in the circle is connected. In our attempt to raise awareness we intentionally place our attention on the various points at the same time so that we don't get lost in just one attention. Placing our attention on three points and then five enables us to be five times more aware than when we are in dreamless sleep. However, since the points are all ultimately connected, they will and do bleed over and onto each other to a certain degree. But those of us who are exceptional at this can place attention onto all five points at once with very little or no perceived overlap. As you know, attention to yourself is a separate point from attention to your object. Just as attention on yourself or the object is separate from your intuition or instinct or what is below you that you cannot perceive with your senses. Your ego or your personality or your emotions or your physical senses are not intuition or instinct. They are two completely different points. The object of your attention is not intuition. The place where you are is not instinct. This is why we designate the perception of the subconscious and the unseen, *what lies beneath*, as the fourth point of attention. But as I said earlier, you will not be able to truly verify that until you also add the fifth. So let's explain that now.

"The fifth point of attention is the beyond, signified as being above. The best way to begin to grasp this point of attention is to first not associate it with any other point. In explaining the fourth point to you, you automatically asked if it is part of the other three. This is a normal response. But the answer is no. All the points are separate even though they are connected. If you are in the East you are not in the West. If you are in the North you are not in the South. But you are still on planet Earth. Ultimately all is connected. In this sense we place our fifth attention in a separate place that can be described as the beyond. The beyond is not your intuition, it is not what you call yourself, it is not any object, circumstance, or place.

"The fifth point is completely dispassionate and indifferent. It can be likened to how the sun or stars or moon would think or feel about us; they do not think or feel anything about us. They are beyond us. We use the analogy *above* simply for understanding purposes and also for practicality in learning. This attention is a point outside of anything that we know. But when we are aware of the reality of this point, we gain perspective of our true essence because it is not influenced at all by who we think we are or even what we do. The fifth point is the so-called companion of the fourth point because, just like the first three points, they only work together. Intuition and instinct are underlying states whose essence is only fully comprehended by awareness of the fifth point of attention, the beyond. Conversely, attention of the beyond is only truly accessed when coupled with the point of attention of what lies beneath."

Jesús added, "It might not appear so to you now, but the fifth point is actually the closest point that we can place our attention on. In this same regard, we can describe the fourth point as the farthest. The fourth point includes awareness that is brought to light through attention or circumstances of life. The fifth attention simply *is*. It is there always just waiting for you to catch it!

"James, there will be many more chances for discussion about these things in the coming days, and it is normal to have questions. I believe tomorrow will be very important to you as you begin to apply your awareness of the five points of attention all together during the light of day, traveling, conversing, sensing, and all that. But for now, my suggestion is to work with the fire for a while. A good task would be to place the pillow and arrows back to pointing to our destination for tomorrow and to feed the fire some more wood."

Jesús looked toward Maria and she added, "Tatewari, our Grandfather Fire, is the best guide for integrating the five attentions. Now that our preliminary explanation of the remaining two points is concluded for the moment, you will no doubt be testing out whether you can perceive and combine all five. The fire can help you because it embodies all five attentions. While working with the fire you place attention on the first point by being aware of how and what *you feel*. Am I warm? Do I feel sleepy? Don't burn myself! Am I confused? Happy? Whatever.

"The fire is an awesome *object* outside of yourself to direct the awareness of your second point of attention. The fire also illuminates the *place* where we are, so our attention is aware of our third point. Awareness of the fourth attention is exuded by the warmth of the fire as it brings forth the energy of the wood that lies within it. There are not many entities or phenomena that bring out the fourth attention of our primal feelings, instinctual knowledge, and intuition more profoundly than fire. And of course the element of fire perfectly reflects indifference and insignificance toward human beings and their affairs; it lets us know clearly that we are not the center of the universe, which is the essence of the fifth attention."

For the rest of that night, I carefully tended the fire while expanding my attention to five attentions and for the first time I truly understood what this practice was about. My primal mind was awakening but not at the expense of my personality or ego. I felt in a state of balance that I had never experienced before and is difficult to put into words. It was like I was one with everything but at the same time myself.

 # Cerro Gordo

The next morning, we hiked to the top of the sacred mountain. Since I grew up and lived most of my life in mountainous regions, I felt more at home in this environment than anywhere else in the Huichol sacred landscape. At first we walked through towering oak trees and as we climbed higher the oaks were replaced with fir and pines. With my attention focused on the five points, I realized that I felt energized even with little sleep because of an unseen energy that permeated these forests. There were lots of squirrels and birds around, deer tracks, and at one point I saw the clear footprint of a mountain lion.

Very close to the top of the mountain, the Huichol arrived at their destination: A rirriki built of piled stones and wood; the house of the ancient ancestor spirits that lived in the sacred place of Cerro Gordo—Hauxamanaka. Compared to other rirrikis I had been to, such as those in Teakata and the one at the top of Cerro Quemado overlooking the peyote fields in Wirikuta, this one appeared to be less used and contained only a few offerings. I got the feeling that not as many Huichol came to this place, but it could have been that the rirriki had been recently cleaned out, either ceremonially by other Huichol or through theft by tewaris. There was no door or any other kind of security for this rirriki, and it could easily be pillaged if someone found it and wanted to take items from inside it.

I really didn't need to ask why this place was special to the Huichol or anyone else for that matter. The view and the scenery, the *place,* was exceptional and held a unique sort of energy or power. As an avid technical rock climber, mountaineer, skier, and snowboarder I had been to hundreds of places that commanded awe-inspiring beauty and majestic views.

But looking to the four directions in this place, I got a sense of the history and of the importance that it represented to the Huichol as their sacred place in the North. The very top of the mountain is the highest point in the Sierra Madre Occidental at around eleven thousand feet. In the area to the South, way below us was the tiny town of San Francisco de Lajas; as I turned to the North, the sky was so incredibly clear I could actually see the top of the mountain Cerro Prieto, around ten thousand feet high but hundreds of miles away.

All around us were sheer rock cliffs and megaliths of rock that towered over the trees and terrain below. In looking around, my eyes caught sight of the rirriki once again. I must have had a curious look in my eyes that Jesús picked up on. Thus he gave a brief explanation of where I was standing in relationship to the Huichol world. I had actually heard this story before but obviously had never been to this sacred site.

Along with dozens of other spiritual traditions and religions, including the Bible religions and native religions, Huichol too have their version of a great flood—the purification of the Earth and its creatures so that a new and more improved world can be born. In this case, the most ancient ancestor, Watákame, is instructed by Nakawé to build a canoe to carry him, a dog (which later becomes human and also his wife), and seeds of the different kinds of corn and squash, along with fire. After the rains subside, Watákame's canoe lands on the high mountain of Cerro Gordo where the rirriki now stands. Together with his wife, Watákame has many children and creates a new race of people—the Huichol. The full tale of Watákame and the flood is much longer and extremely detailed.

Inside the rirriki was a small offering that someone had made depicting Watakamé's canoe. So for the Huichol, coming to this place was like coming back to where they all started. I would find out a lot more about this sacred place later but for now the Huichol occupied themselves with announcing their arrival by blowing their bull horns, gathering firewood, and generally preparing for the night.

With night closing in, the sacred fire was kindled and Maria and Marcelino began preparing dried peyote by crushing it into powder so it could be stirred into water and drunk. While watching them, a question came to mind and I asked Jesús, "How do the five attentions relate to the peyote?"

"The five attentions expand normal awareness to get to your true essence. The hikuri is for traveling. But being aware of your essence is the way to access the true power of the hikuri. You have had some success in meeting and traveling with the hikuri before because you had some sense of your essence and because, in your own way, you come clean with your heart. Most tewaris and even some Huichol don't experience the meeting with the spirit of the hikuri in a tangible and productive sense. They can see the magical colors and symbols but they don't actually meet the spirit.

"It's like sitting up in the seats of a big stadium and seeing someone standing in the middle of the field down below and far away. You see someone is there but without binoculars you can't tell who it is. Then if you have *tri-noculars,* awareness of three points of attention, you can see who it is but you are still not there with them. By being one with your true essence, five points of attention, you can jump down onto the field and be right next to the spirit, and then hug, feel, kiss, and speak to the spirit.

"This of course is just a way of putting into words something that is unexplainable. The hikuri grabs your attention and unveils to you what you are able to comprehend. Nothing more and nothing less. The hikuri is most like the fifth attention, the above and beyond. The hikuri doesn't care about ego or personality or subject or object or place. This spirit that opens doors [nierika] to unfathomable realms only admits the true essence of exceptional awareness. All others are left outside waiting and wondering if they can come inside and explore the many floors and rooms of the mansion."

"The mansion?"

"Yes! The mansion is a metaphor for the multilevel kingdom of countless rooms of awareness and perception outside of our everyday consciousness. Also known as *la gloria* [the glory] or *el paraíso* [paradise].* This is the destination of the marakáme when we sing. It is through the plumes of sacred birds, the blood of ancestor deer, the water of heavenly springs, the scent and color of magical flowers, that la gloria is manifest in our physical dimension.

"As human beings alive in the physical world, we can't live all the time in la gloria so we incorporate the things that are most filled with la gloria in our ceremonies to help us enter when we knock on the doors of the mansion. The plumed muvieri, the blood of ancestor deer, the water from the sacred springs, the divine cactus of Wirikuta, you can see us always using them to unlock the mysteries of the mansion. If we don't come with gifts when we arrive at the front door, we just look like beggars and we get sent away. Maybe if they are in a good mood, those in the mansion will throw some crumbs for us to eat as they send us away.

"I have been to lots of places in the mansion but there are still doors that remain locked for me. To enter through the doors of those rooms, to unlock them and go inside, I must become more exceptional in my awareness, in my thoughts, and in my actions. The deeper I go into my true essence while walking through life the further I travel into la gloria.

"The challenging part about visiting la gloria is coming back and living your normal life of having food to eat, a home and family, work and responsibilities. Here we have to make the conscious effort to be true to our essence and live exceptional lives. This is how we express la gloria. Our actions, our thoughts, even the clothes we wear demonstrate our level of awareness to la gloria."

---

*I have heard on many occasions from different Huichol that they went to paradise and back when referring to the pilgrimage to Wirikuta and the peyote visions acquired there.

Although enthralled with what Jesús was explaining, I was getting more and more distracted by Maria, who had been chuckling to herself for the last few minutes, ever since Jesús had mentioned the mansion, and she seemed to be holding back a really good belly laugh. When I asked her what was so funny she turned her face away.

"She thinks it's too vulgar to tell you and she's embarrassed," Marcelino said.

"Come on, Maria, tell me," I implored like a little kid.

Maria laughed at my tone and said, "Okay I was just laughing because when Grandfather was talking to you about the mansion I thought about the ant."

"What ant?" I asked confused.

"She's talking about the ant in the mansion," Marcelino replied. "I'll tell you the story."

For the next few minutes Maria, Marcelino, Rafael, and Jesús broke into a hilarious (to them) debate about who should get to tell me this particular story. In the end they agreed to share the tale together. Maria started first because she thought it was the best part and girls never got to say it.

"One day Maxakwaxi was sitting on the toilet doing his business in one of the beautiful bathrooms in the mansion."

"I think he was reading a book!" Jesús added with mirth.

"Out of the corner of his eye, he saw this tiny little ant walking around on the windowsill right next to him below the window that looked out onto the world," Maria continued.

"He was a little bit surprised that an ant would be in the magnificent mansion. Without really thinking too much about it he stuck out a finger and like nothing he squashed the tiny ant and went back to what he was doing."

The Huichol all pretended like the story was over. I was just about to protest when Jesús added, "The ant in the story is a tewari that eats hikuri and sneaks into the mansion looking for crumbs."

I was more confused than before when Rafael chimed in, "I'm a cute, black puppy dog with a white tail! When the marakáme opens the door, I slip inside and run around the rooms sniffing. Most of the time when I run into Maxakwaxi, I just wag my tail and act all friendly and he just pets my head and massages my ears. But when I'm bad and shit on the carpet, he yells at me and kicks me out. But at least I'm not an ant and don't get squashed."

The Huichol all rolled with laughter.

"All of us here are still animals except Grandfather Jesús," Maria explained. "Right now I'm a butterfly. I fly around in the gardens outside the mansion and sometimes I fly around inside when a window gets open. Marcelino is a mean cat, he catches mice in the mansion and for that reason Maxakwaxi feeds him. Grandfather Jesús is an exceptional marakáme. He walks around the house just like you see him here. He wears his own clothes, carries his morals, and has on his hat adorned with muvieris."

Rafael chimed in, "He even has his own bedroom where he takes naps and has dreams in his comfortable bed. Some say he even has his own private bathroom all of sparkling white tile!"

The laughter continued until Jesús finally calmed everyone down and addressed me, "James, the point here is that first of all most people never even know the mansion exists. Some believe it is real and try to find it but never do. Others find it but never make it inside because they don't knock loud enough. Their knock is like a tiny tap on the front door. Like when a fly runs into it. Then sometimes a person eats hikuri and sneaks into the mansion as a little bug like an ant. But of course a little bug cannot explore a giant mansion and so it either just dies or gets squashed.

"What we are attempting to teach you is how to arrive at the mansion and knock on the door with confidence and walk around free to explore the vast library of knowledge stored on the shelves."

Maria brought forth in reverence the mask and antlers of the deer she was carrying in one of her morals. She then looked directly into my eyes and I knew she was asking me a silent question. At once I was carried back to the memory of her taking in the last breaths of the deer.

I had not asked Maria about why she had done that, although I was supremely curious about her actions. Jesús calmly explained to me that this sacred mountain in the North was a place where some of the exceptional ancestors came after the last time they died. In this case an exceptional ancestor, now incarnated as a deer, was one of Maria's guides in the spirit world. He was an ancient marakáme who was gifting part of his iyari to Maria so she could become a marakáme too and move up to the final floor in the mansion.

"The final floor of the mansion?" I asked.

Maria answered me herself, "We call it the mansion because that is what it looks and feels like on the first and second floors. The bottom floors are a huge place filled with souls. The mansion is actually more like a pyramid that has five floors. A soul's awareness of his or her true essence determines what floor they will reach when they die. The bottom floors have many guides who usher the other souls to where they will be next. Most of the people living on Earth have only been to the bottom two floors. Only the truly exceptional souls ever get to look out from the top. It is a much smaller place at the top of the pyramid."

"So what determines placement on the different floors?" I asked.

"The manner in which you conduct yourself, which is determined by your level of awareness to your essence," Jesús replied and continued.

"Most people arrive into the world from the first two floors because they are not aware of their true essence. Some souls have even lived thousands of lives here on Earth but are still unaware. This lack of awareness is the root cause of humanity's problems. Unaware of their true essence they cause wars, rape, and steal from each other, and so on. But there are moments in the lives of every soul when they have the chance to change. Whether or not they decide to listen more to their essence determines where they end up next.

"This is very important for you, James, because I have spoken to the ancestors and it is time for you to embrace your essence and gain access to the next floor. Maria, Marcelino, and Rafael are in a similar situation. All of you have awareness of your essence to make the decision to go even further. But only your actions can elevate you. It takes conscious effort to be an exceptional soul. It is very hard for people to hear that they are not exceptional. That they do not know their true essence. That they have never been to the upper floors of the mansion."

With extreme trepidation I asked Jesús, "What floor do you think I am on?"

Jesús looked to the jicareros and Rafael answered, "By your actions we all know you have come here from the third floor. We don't know how many times you have come back from that floor but we all believe you are ready to advance. Marcelino and I have also come from the third floor but hope to now reach the fourth also. Maria has already reached the fourth and is striving for the top where the most exceptional ancestors are waiting for her."

Marcelino added, "We are very surprised to meet a tewari from the third floor that is ready to reach the fourth. Jesús tells us he has met only one before and none of the rest of us here has ever met a tewari such as you. Jesús says there are seven billion souls on the Earth right now. That is a number I honestly can't comprehend. Almost all of them have come from the first two floors. Some of them are new or very young souls. Others are souls that simply don't advance and keep returning from the same floor.

"With attention, reaching the third floor is not so difficult even though most people never get there. Being aware of your true essence and conducting yourself with compassion for others should just be natural. That is the way we were born. But it can't remain that way when people grow up in cultures and religions that persecute each other. Unfortunately most new and young souls arriving from the lower floors are born surrounded by others from the same level so it is difficult to advance. This is also because these places of birth are governed by very old souls that have not advanced. Very old souls not advancing through hundreds or thousands of lifetimes become tyrannical leaders of the less-developed souls. These leaders seem advanced but they are not. As displayed by their actions, they are still immature. When or if each of us comes back from the fourth floor we will come with the responsibility and potential to be guides for other souls."

"What happens at the fifth level?" I asked.

"We can come back as crystals or whales or even deer if we want to. Or we may choose to come back as a marakáme like Grandfather Jesús. The other option is to not return at all and become a guide for others in the spirit world," Maria answered.

Through various other conversations pertaining to Huichol ritual during the next couple of hours, I was informed that this would be a very special night for Maria. With the aid of the antlers and blood of the ancient ancestor, Jesús and Maria would enter trance and while singing Jesús would lead Maria to the spirit world and attempt to guide her to the fifth floor of the pyramid.

The Huichol all seemed to be in an intense state of concentration and awareness of the five attentions as they made prayer offerings by decorating small bamboo arrows and jicaras that they had brought with them. I was instructed on how to decorate my prayer arrows with the different colors of pigment they had brought—the different colors representing my attention and prayers to be offered to the ancestors of this sacred site.

With the offerings complete, they were reverently placed in the rirriki and then blessed with deer blood and sacred water by Jesús as he chanted prayers while we all drank a frothy mixture of peyote and water. Marcelino and Rafael played their instruments for the ancestors at the top of the mountain while Jesús conducted his lengthy blessing.

I had asked through my prayer arrows for vision into how I could do my part as service to the ancestors, humanity, and the planet. I wasn't disappointed. While Jesús and Maria sang throughout the night on their journey to the spirit world I had visions of many things. But the first and absolutely most astonishing thing that happened to me was right in the beginning of the night—just as I was starting to feel the spirit of the peyote entering into my awareness, I heard the snap of a twig somewhere behind me. I turned and looked away from the fire into the darkness but saw nothing. I remained peering into the dark because I was sure I had heard something. As my eyes slowly adjusted, I could faintly see the outline of a deer standing in the trees.

Immediately I knew I had to expand my attention to the five points and when I did I clearly saw what appeared to be a blue deer, one of the most sacred ancestors of the Huichol. But this was no ethereal peyote-induced vision. This was an actual live deer. I caught my rational mind thinking that it must be a rare albino deer, which I had seen in photos but never personally encountered before.

The deer did not look directly at me and with a wag of his tail he walked into the darkness. The last I saw of him was that unique wag, a sort of quick swooshing back and forth of the deer's tail and then he was gone. I turned back to the fire and it seemed like that swooshing of the deer's tail was like a shot or bell signifying the beginning of an event because after the deer swooshed his tail at me, my night of visions dramatically began.

I won't get into a lengthy narrative of my visions but what I was basically given was a dual version of current life on planet Earth. In the beginning, I was left sobbing after being shown all the suffering and wars going on. Then I was shown lots of amazing and beautiful things like migrating wales, the hatching of a bird (which I had the feeling was some sort of hawk), clouds majestically floating through the sky, and the intensely colorful formations of new galaxies in the omniverse.

My personal visions ended with me coming alive as a peyote flower in Wirikuta. It was an amazing experience to blossom and release my pollen. I was astounded that I was aware of being each of the tiny grains of pollen. But the magnificent feeling of the vision turned dramatically as each speck of pollen fell to the ground and died. There were no other flowers around to pollenate. At the end of my vision I felt spent, like I had just lived through a thousand deaths.

I spent the rest of the night sitting with my legs held tightly to my chest and listening to the singing of Jesús and Maria. In the morning, the Huichol seemed pretty spent, too, but they were in good spirits. I spoke to Jesús about my visions and he seemed very pleased. All the Huichol were amazed by my story of seeing the deer and the swooshing of his tail. They didn't seem to care in the least whether the deer was physical or visionary because all agreed and were excited because I had encountered Maxakwaxi—Great-Grandfather Deer Tail. According to them, I had knocked on the door exceptionally enough that with a swoosh of his tail Maxakwaxi opened it and let me in. They all agreed that was the most significant part of my night and a very good sign that my soul was advancing.

Maria also had an exceptional night and at dawn she immediately began making a complex drawing on a small piece of wood with beeswax and yarn. She excitedly explained to me that she had traveled to the upper floor and one of the women ancestors gave her a new design for her weaving. According to Jesús this was the most exceptional way to acquire designs because they come straight from the ancestors. By obtaining this sacred design, Maria had taken the next step in becoming a master weaver.*

While talking with Jesús, he was also very interested in my vision of being a peyote flower in Wirikuta and was disturbed by what I told him. He said that he too had had a vision in Wirikuta and that we should make the journey to the home of the peyote right away. There were only two more things left to do before leaving. Maria needed to finish her design because she was going to leave it in the rirriki, and Jesús wanted to visit one more sacred site on the way down the mountain.

I was surprised when Maria actually did leave her newly acquired design in the rirriki of this remote place. When I asked her about it she explained that it was customary for weavers to share their designs in this way and that she hoped another weaver would come and take it and copy it in order for it to be used by more people. She said that in sacred sites when a woman left one of her original designs, she could take one that someone else had left. When I asked her if she would

---

*Huichol women who are master weavers achieve similar, or in some cases even greater, respect in the community to marakámes.

remember what it looked like, she just smiled at me and replied, "What do you think?"

Jesús began leading us down the mountain by a different way than we had climbed up. When I asked him about the change of course—same direction, different route—he said that he had a vision in the night of a place of an ancient ancestor, incarnated as a white-tail hawk, and he wanted to go there to collect feathers to make muvieris.

We arrived at the top of a sheer cliff and while peering down Jesús seemed extremely pleased. "This is the place!" he said excitedly.

Looking over the edge, I didn't see anything except rock and a few trees sticking out. Jesús whispered to me, as if sharing a secret, that there was a nest in an alcove below us that we couldn't see. We would have to walk around and get under the cliff to find the feathers, which indeed we did.

To my amazement when we finally reached the bottom I could clearly see a nest built high up in the cliff, and from the amount of poop stains on the rocks it appeared that particular nesting place may have been used many times throughout the years. The Huichol were giddy with excitement as one by one we began to find feathers. The jicareros and I each found one suitable feather and Jesús found two, totaling six feathers. While we were looking, Jesús explained that the markings on the feathers were similar to the design Maria just made in that they contain coded messages.

"These messages make up songs that the marakáme sings. The white-tail hawk is the bird representative of the sacred place of Hauxamanaka. Other birds such as the red-tailed hawk, eagle, turkey, and some coastal birds have their own sacred sites. Through the muvieri I will make with these feathers I will be able to sing through the ancestors that dwell here in the North." He very reverently opened his takwatsi and slipped them in with a smile saying, "We have plenty of time to make some fine muvieris on our way to Wirikuta."

Wirikuta

The drive from the Huichol sacred place of the North to the sacred place in the East took around ten hours, mostly on good roads and even highways after we left the mountains behind us. Upon arriving at the area of the sacred peyote desert, the roads deteriorated quickly.

As is traditional, we stopped at Tatei Matinieri, the sacred spring at the edge of the peyote desert, and also Tuimayau, the sacred spring much closer to the peyote. These sites are visited by all Huichol arriving in these lands, and I had been taken to these springs each time I traveled there. In each place, offerings and prayers were given, water was collected in small bottles, and Jesús blessed us with these living waters by pouring water on our heads while chanting prayers for life and health. In each case, Maria blessed Jesús as well. Also, in Tuimayau we collected some pieces of a root from a sacred plant called uxa, which is yellow in color and used to make paint for ceremonial face painting.

It is significant to note that our small group now had with us sacred water from all five major sacred sites related to the Center, South, West, North, and now East. The jicareros had brought with them water from the south (Xapawiyeme), and the West (Haramara). Jesús and I had collected spring water from the Center (Teakata), and our group had now together collected water from the sacred spring of the North (Hauxamanaka) and those of the East (Tatei Matinieri and Tuimayau). It cannot be overstated how important these sacred waters are to the Huichol. The Huichol who still live in the core of their territory in the Sierra have such an extreme reliance on rain to grow their crops that the bringing of rain is a central activity in most Huichol ceremonies in the Sierra. By having water collected from the cardinal directions, the marakámes can sing to them to bring the rain, which is vital to their lives.

The sun was going down as we drove the dusty, rut-filled dirt road deeper into the desert. Jesús seemed to be deep in thought and no one had spoken in quite a while. The light was failing quickly and I began to wonder where we would spend the night when suddenly Jesús told me to stop the truck.

He pointed up ahead and off to the right. "There are people in the chaparral over there."

I looked closely to where he was pointing and saw a flicker of light up ahead. "Someone has a fire going," Jesús added. He looked over at me with a grin. "Let's park and check it out."

We all got out and began walking toward the light that was about a quarter mile away. It was fully dark now with little moonlight but neither I, nor the much more experienced Huichol, had trouble walking in the chaparral. I asked Jesús what he had in mind, and he said he just wanted to get closer and have a look to see who it was without them seeing us. From his tone and expression, and from his previous displays of visionary expertise, I had the distinct feeling he already knew who it might be.

"They could be Huichol but I doubt it." He added, "It is not the time of year for pilgrimages. More than likely they are people coming here for the peyote or other cactus. Maybe they are the hippie types but they could also be some poachers. The poachers can be dangerous men, so let's be very careful and quiet."

As we got closer, I could make out the form of a vehicle in the light of a small campfire but couldn't see or hear any people. Jesús motioned for us to stay and silently gave the one-minute sign with his index finger and slipped away.

Over a half hour went by before Jesús finally came back. "There are three young people over there. Two men and a girl. One man sounds like a local Mexican and I think the other two are gringos. The gringos speak Spanish but not too well and I heard them all speaking English. I couldn't really hear what they were talking about. They are just sitting by the fire and drinking beer but they don't appear to be drunk."

"So what do you want to do?" I asked.

Jesús thought for a second then said, "Why don't you go over and start up a conversation? I'd like to know what they are doing here but I'm guessing I already know. If they see us all they might get scared and try to run away—or maybe something worse. They don't look very dangerous to me but you never know."

Looking at the marakáme, Jesús, and the three other Huichol in their embroidered regalia, carrying machetes and long knives the thought occurred to me that if I was here in the desert at night, I probably wouldn't be comfortable with them walking into my campsite at night. "What do you want me to say?" I asked.

"You're good at talking, you'll figure it out. Go on now. We'll wait for you here," Jesús said rather impatiently.

I left my things with my friends and began walking toward the fire because the last thing I wanted was to get robbed. As I walked silently I wondered what I would say when I got there. The sun had recently gone down so it wasn't real late and one gringo shouldn't feel like that much of an intrusion. But that was simply my perspective. Who knows what they would think.

I stepped into the ring of light made by the fire. Like Jesús said, there were three people who appeared to be in their midtwenties sitting by the fire having some beers. I also noticed a pile of peyote tops sitting next to the stone ring they had made for the fire. When I entered, all three jumped up in surprise but after a few moments of speaking in English, "Hey, how's it goin?" and all that, they relaxed a bit. I didn't want to come right out and ask them what they were doing in the sacred (and supposedly government-protected) peyote desert, so I told them a little white lie—that my truck got a flat on the dirt road a way back and I saw their fire. I quickly introduced myself and they all shook hands with me. I mustn't have seemed like a threat as they were all friendly toward me, although the Mexican guy seemed a little wary.

Over the next few minutes, I learned that Sage and Michael were a couple from Santa Fe, New Mexico, and Carlos was local to Real de Catorce—the dusty old mining town that sits up in the mountain above the peyote desert and in recent years has become alive again through the tourism trade. Though the Mexican government officially condemns the harvesting of the psychotropic peyote cactus by anyone outside the Huichol community for religious reasons, Real de Catorce's website advertises the town as the place of the "pilgrimage of people of all ages and nationalities . . . who travel thousands of miles to arrive at this sacred site and experience a mystical communion with the magical cactus." Every year there are more and more Mexican "guides" in Real de Catorce offering to take people into the desert for experiences with the peyote, which of course is against the law.

It was pretty obvious to me that Carlos had brought the two Americans to the desert for peyote consumption and perhaps harvesting— probably for a handsome fee. Surprisingly to me, Carlos seemed very at ease considering they were all involved in an illegal activity and I was wondering when he was going to ask me what I was doing there. But I didn't have to wait long as Sage enthusiastically broached the subject by asking if I was there hunting for peyote.

"Not exactly," I replied. "What about you guys?"

The three of them looked at each other and Carlos answered. "We are doing a peyote ceremony here tomorrow night with some more people. We came early to set things up."

Seeing this as my opportunity, I told them that I was with some Huichol friends who had brought me there.

Carlos stiffened a little at that and said, "You are here with Huicholitos? How odd. Where are they?"

It was my turn to stiffen a little. Not because of what he asked so much as how he asked it. The term *Huicholito* was a diminutive word used by some Mexicans for the Huichol. Literally it means "little Huichol," signifying that the Indians were lesser-class citizens. It was a term I'd always despised and one that I'm sure my friends on this trip would not be happy to hear. The Huichol I was traveling with were certainly not Huicholitos in any sense of the word.

"Well, my friends are waiting for me back at the truck," I replied. "They're a little shy. But now that I see we are all friends here I can go get them. If you really want to learn about the peyote, these are the experts."

Carlos balked at this idea, saying, "No, that's okay, we're fine." But Sage got all excited and said that she was hoping to someday meet some Huichol and that it was a dream for her to do so. Michael agreed, so without delay I stood up and announced that I'd go get them and be right back.

I quickly found the group and filled them in. Jesús wanted to go back to the truck and get our things before going to meet them. Half an hour later we were at their fire. After some quick introductions, Jesús said they would go get some more firewood and the Huichol disappeared into the night.

All three of the tewaris were very curious about the small group of Indians. I told them that Jesús was a well-respected marakáme from the Sierra de Jalisco and an expert in the ritual use of peyote and that the others were jicareros serving as temple members. Carlos immediately seemed less at ease and asked if Jesús would tell on them for taking the peyote. My answer was the truth—I really didn't know. In that moment I guess Carlos felt like he needed to redeem himself as the leader of the group and stated that there was nothing the Huicholitos could do. "We can be here if we want to be here. This land is not only sacred to the Huichol. The peyote is here for anyone who wants to learn from it."

Even though from a metaphysical standpoint that may be true, from a legal perspective he was completely wrong, and I'm sure he knew it. On previous pilgrimages with Huichol groups my name was included in the official documents as a sponsor of the pilgrimage, but in the eyes of the government I was still technically not allowed to harvest or ingest the peyote even though my Huichol companions encouraged it. The only legal rights I obtained from being an official part of the pilgrimage was that I was allowed to be with the Huichol while they were in possession of the sacred cactus. In this case, we had an official paper stamped by the traditional authorities for what we were doing. But because I was with Jesús, I kept my mouth shut about the whole legality issue until I saw what he would do. They came back with fuel for the fire a few minutes later and Marcelino and Rafael took over the care of the fire.

There were a tense few minutes as everyone sat quietly. But it wasn't long before Rafael grabbed a large peyote top from the tewari's rather large pile. He began cleaning it by pulling the white tufts from the center and then started slicing it into segments with his knife. "Is this why you are here? For the peyote?" he asked gruffly.

"It can help you see magical things if you treat it nice. Or it can deliver you straight to hell if you don't," Marcelino added.

"Or you can puke your guts up and feel really sick all night if you don't confess right," Maria chimed in.

"If you are really lucky, you can see Tamatz Kahullumary, the blue deer, dancing in the fire," Rafael continued while cleaning and cutting another peyote top.

"Or Kahullumary can trick you and when you go take a piss the *vibora de cascabel* [rattlesnake] that guards the peyote will bite you," Marcelino added once more.

"Sometimes Kahullumary will sneak up behind you and breathe warm air on your neck until you get very sleepy and fall over and hit your head on a rock," Maria chimed in again.

For the next ten minutes or so, the three jicareros took turns describing what could happen with the peyote. Some situations were funny and others deadly serious. The tewaris said nothing. Jesús and I simply enjoyed the show until Rafael was done preparing a quantity of the peyote and all went silent again.

Jesús addressed the tewaris in a concerned voice. "You do realize you are breaking the law by cutting these peyotes out from the ground? Tell me why you would do such a thing?"

Sage was the first to answer and said that they had read and heard many wonderful things about the power of the peyote to grant visions and they wanted to try it for themselves. Michael added in a somewhat shaky voice that they were much honored to get to meet the Huichol in the sacred desert. Sage and Michael seemed like nice and intelligent people to me. I'm pretty sure that when people come down from Real de Catorce venturing into the desert, ninety-nine out of one hundred times they don't run into a group of Huichol. It was either great or bad luck for this couple. The night was still young.

"And what about you?" Jesús questioned Carlos after it seemed he wasn't going to volunteer to speak.

"People come to me to bring them here."

"You mean people *pay* you to bring them here," Rafael said, while slowly cleaning off his knife.

"Sure, why not?" Carlos replied defensively. "I have been leading peyote ceremonies for many years. I am very famous for what I do and people come from around the world to see me. Unlike you I was born in this state. You come from far away but claim ownership of all the peyote. I only take the tops and teach people to do the same so the plants will come back. Unfortunately I have to be more careful than you and not get caught by the federales. It's really not fair."

After another long silence, Jesús stood up and said cheerily, "Okay! Then let's eat some peyote and talk friendly some more with each other and see what Grandfather Fire and Kahullumary have to say!"

Carlos stood too and replied, "We weren't planning to eat any peyote until tomorrow night when the rest of our friends come."

Catching on to what Jesús had in mind, Rafael added, "Well, how often do you get to meet the peyote spirit in the presence of a powerful marakáme in the middle of Wirikuta? You could charge your clients triple for that!"

Everyone in the small group laughed at that, except Carlos. Sage added, "No offense to Carlos, but I agree with Rafael. Why wait until tomorrow night when we have this once-in-a-lifetime opportunity to learn from a master?"

Michael agreed but Jesús quickly countered, "The ancestors and the peyote are in control here, not me. I'm just a humble servant. No one is master of the peyote."

"Then it's settled," Rafael said. "We'll go and hunt a few more deer."*

The three jicareros took out their long knives and Jesús blessed them with his muvieris. The tewaris had collected more than enough peyote for all of us but I'm guessing that the Huichol preferred to ingest peyote that they had hunted and captured themselves in a more traditional way. Half an hour later, they returned with a few more peyote tops and began preparing them. Maria commented to Carlos that he had picked a nice spot. There were lots of peyotes all around. Carlos simply nodded his head yes in reply. He had become seriously silent.

When the jicareros were done preparing the peyote and divided about half of it up into plastic cups the tewaris had brought, Jesús explained that before meeting the peyote in Wirikuta the heart must be cleaned. To the Huichol this means speaking clearly into the fire all of your sexual partners. I have been more than once with groups including first-time pilgrims to Wirikuta and this procedure can sometimes take most of the night. When a person is confessing and gets stuck or embarrassed or stops talking for whatever reason, one of the leaders whips them (not very hard, just encouragingly) with a piece of rope or a thin, long stick.

The Huichol say that the better one confesses, the cleaner they will be—the better to receive the peyote. It is very important not to forget a sexual partner while confessing or even worse to intentionally omit

---

*The flesh of deer, peyote, and corn form a sacred triangle in Huichol cosmology and one is often referred to as the other. Especially in Wirikuta, the peyote is equated with ancestor deer.

them because you don't want others to hear. This can be extremely difficult for pilgrims of small communities who have lived and known each other their entire lives. There may be many secrets among the group. But Huichol take this with dead seriousness. They would rather deal with the personal repercussions of someone hearing something they don't like than meet the peyote with an unclean heart, which is seriously dangerous to them.

Jesús asked who was going first. No one said anything so I addressed Grandfather Fire saying that I was in Wirikuta years before and I had confessed my rather long list at that time. Each time after that, I confessed. Since my last time confessing in Wirikuta, I had not had sexual relations with anyone. I explained to Grandfather that I was not being celibate on purpose but rather I was being careful with my sexual energy and had not found anyone since my last confession that I wanted to share that with. My first confession was long. Knowing beforehand that I was going to have to do it, I made a list to bring with me so I wouldn't forget anyone, but since then I have been much more aware of where I give my energy.

The jicareros and Jesús were all either celibate since their last confession or were faithful to their wives so no names were given to Grandfather from the five of us. Sage said that she would go next and Jesús directed her to stand up, speak in a clear loud voice, and begin by saying, "Grandfather Fire, here in Wirikuta, in front of you and all my companions [this includes the unseen ancestors], I have these sexual encounters to confess to you so that I am clean."

Sage repeated Jesús's words and began stating names. After each name the group repeated the name back to her. She had around ten people, but I really wasn't counting. Sage seemed to do a good job and became quite emotional toward the end of her list, and I noticed Michael got fidgety around that same time. According to Huichol tradition, Jesús had tied a knot into a thin piece of rope for each person Sage had revealed. When she was finished, Jesús showed her the knotted rope and with some words he ceremoniously placed it into the fire.

Afterward he asked, "Who's next?" But neither of the two men spoke up.

Jesús told the tewaris that it was a bad idea to meet the peyote in Wirikuta without a clean heart. Michael was obviously not comfortable with the idea and finally said, "I'm not doing it. I see no reason to talk about my sexual partners. I have always had consensual sex and I don't think there is anything bad about that. I don't need to confess my sexual life because I have done nothing wrong."

Carlos also declined, stating that he knew the peyote spirit very well and did not see the need to do something as silly as confess his sexual life. I could tell the jicareros were concerned and somewhat bewildered by these men. My guess was that Michael had something to hide from Sage and that Carlos was just being arrogant. Having confessed on many occasions with the Huichol, I have given this subject a lot of thought over the years. My opinion is that this act of confessing is so ingrained in their culture that whether or not the spirit of the peyote actually does something bad to them if they do not confess well, they will cause themselves to have a "bad trip" if they know they didn't do it well. This is especially true for the first-time pilgrims, called *matawámes,* who have never confessed before and so may have many people to declare. Promiscuity is far from unknown to the Huichol.

This seems to be not as strong a motivation for people who do not grow up learning and expecting this type of confession. But I do believe that getting clean with yourself before ingesting the peyote or any other psychotropic substance can go a long way to having a pleasant trip. For tewaris (including myself) this could mean giving to the Grandfather Fire anything you need to get rid of, not just sexual stuff. For me this is different from the sins of Catholic confession because it could be anything—like drinking too much, cheating on your taxes, feeling guilty for not calling your mom enough, fighting with your partner—any of which are not sins but rather situations that may ultimately cause a decrease in the quality of your life. If your mind is in chaos about certain things, then psychotropics will often amplify the chaos and that can be very dangerous to your mental health.

Since it was clear the confession period was over, Jesús had everyone stand and one by one he blessed us with his chanting of prayers for us and with his muvieris. His blessing is guided by a small, round mirror attached to one of the muvieris in his bundle. With the aid of the mirror, or nierika,* he can look into a person's heart, their iyari, and know what blessings to request from the peyote for each person. The final part of the blessing for each individual was for him to place our first segment of peyote into our mouth after first touching it to our wrists, heart, both eyes, and lips.

"So, Carlos," Jesús said casually as we all sat down around the fire after the blessings were complete. "You say you have been doing peyote ceremonies for many years. Can you tell me what you do in those ceremonies? You are very passionate that it should be legal for you to take peyote. I am just curious as to what you do with it."

With an air of reluctance, Carlos replied, "Well, first we bring the people here and show them how to find the peyote and how to properly cut the peyote top from the root so it can grow back. Later we show them how to clean it and prepare it for making tea. We make the tea until nighttime and then we drink it while saying prayers. After that, throughout the night we sometimes drum or sing or dance. Everyone has their own personal experience, you know? As the leader, I watch out for everyone. If they are having trouble I help them. Basically I help the people to have a personal experience with the peyote."

Rafael distributed the filled cups of sliced peyote to each person, and we began chewing on our second piece. Carlos said that he didn't usually give people the fresh peyote, or eat it himself, because it is so difficult to eat. The extremely bitter taste makes it difficult for people to get enough of the peyote into their system. He preferred to make a tea so it's easier to ingest.

"We will also sometimes make a tea from the dry powder," Jesús replied. "Or simply mix it with water or the sacred corn beverage. But not here in Wirikuta. Not here where it is fresh and so tasty! We only

---

*As noted in the glossary, *nierika* can have many meanings to the Huichol.

dry it because it does not stay fresh forever. Here in Wirikuta we eat the sweet, fresh flesh and the iyari of the blue deer, Kahullumary. Through his iyari we receive the messages and knowledge of our ancestors. They give me my songs and answer my questions. Through the union with the iyari of Kahullumary it is possible to connect this sacred place with all the other sacred places and the ancestors that dwell in those places— the Mothers and Fathers that give us life. Coming here to Wirikuta is only one part of a much larger tradition of honoring the ancestors, learning our place in the world, and transforming chaos into order. We make many sacrifices to show our respect and desire to be one with our ancestors, to transform into gods, if only temporarily.

"It is true we travel a long way to get here, as you say. And during that route we sacrifice. We don't eat, we sleep very little, we don't have sex or drink alcohol or eat salt. We do everything we can to focus and allow nothing to distract us. And we make offerings to the ancestors as a form of reciprocity with them. You cannot expect to receive without offering. Part of our offering as a culture is to keep alive the traditions of our ancestors in all the sacred places, especially the five major ones. Wirikuta is only one. That is one reason we don't live here like you do. We live in the Center, this place is the East. If we lived here and were just able to come here every day and eat peyote and sell it to people and neglect our homes and the other sacred places there would be no balance. Eventually we would just become crazy and die.

"We do not claim ownership of the peyote as you say. We do not claim ownership of this land. The jicareros come here once a year or maybe once every two years for a few days to be with the sacred places here and the peyote and take some back with us to where we live. Before now, when people who have no tradition regarding peyote take it for financial gain, there was no need for protecting this place. Now it has to be protected from those that will destroy it and later not really care that it is gone. You may have been born close to this desert but I can see it is not really in your heart. You have not yet met the true spirit of the peyote and you have no traditions to help you. Your ancestors do not live here. That is not any fault of yours. But you are charging people money to come here and take peyote and that is not right. Is it yours to sell? If you just want to help people know the peyote why don't you bring them here for free?"

While Jesús and Carlos were talking, the three jicareros quietly took up a friendly conversation with Sage and Michael. Their Spanish was not good but it was enough and it is amazing how much language we can share without actual words.

Carlos sat quiet for a while and seemed to be holding back his anger toward Jesús. Then through clenched teeth he pointed at me. "So what about him? He is not Huichol. He has no ancestors here either. Is it just fine for him to be here taking peyote and not me?"

Jesús chuckled and I felt like he was holding back a really good laugh. He didn't mind laughing wholeheartedly at me, but it seemed he did possess a little bit of restraint with strangers. "You and James are not the same, Carlos. You are here to *make* money from this sacred place. James *spends* and donates money and resources to help protect it. He profits too, but it's spiritual profit. It is heart profit. Maybe because of this or maybe not, I'm not perfectly sure yet, but for whatever reason our ancestors speak to him and that's why he's here. That's why he is with us here in one of our sacred places. You could basically say that the reason James and we Huichol are here tonight is because of *you*."

Carlos sat back and digested Jesús's words. The two Americans were trying to chew and swallow their final slices of peyote with the support of the jicareros, who had finished theirs in just a few minutes. I was almost done eating mine but, even after having eaten it many times before, it was still not easy for me, either. Carlos was having a hard time as well. Jesús was patiently looking into the fire, having already relished his slices.

When all the tewaris had finished their peyote, Jesús asked Sage, Michael, and Carlos if they would like some advice from Kahullumary on how to spend this night. All of them including Carlos said yes and Jesús began.

"First it would be good for all three of you to say *nineviery* with us to the Grandfather Fire and feed the Grandfather with a piece of wood. As you can see we have rearranged your fire from chaos to order. We do this by intentionally placing the food for Tatéwari in a specific way instead of willy-nilly, every which way. The way we do this is to point the food, the sticks, the *flechas* [arrows] in the direction of our attention. We put a bigger log on the bottom, perpendicular to the direction of our flechas to hold them like a pillow. In this way all our flechas are pointing in the same direction. Right now we are pointing them to the place where the Father Sun first emerged out of a cave, *Pariteká,* in the mountain, Reu'unar, you can see in the distance, very close to Real de Catorce, and the rirriki, our shrine for offerings, that is on the top of the mountain. That is where we will go tomorrow. After tomorrow, we will point our arrows to where we go next. If we are not going anywhere soon, we usually point our arrows to the East for the Father Sun.

"In this ritual, before the hikuri, or peyote, arrives at our iyari we make clear to the ancestors why we are here. In other words we don't want any misunderstandings with the powers around us so we simply tell them what's going on and we make offerings. Offerings can be anything in your heart you want to give. After you have spoken to Grandfather why you are here, what you would like to receive, and you made one or more offerings, then place a stick of wood, your flecha, on the pillow and pointing toward the place of the Father Sun. Throughout the night if you need strength or to lighten up your visions or thoughts then follow the flechas to the place of the Father Sun for help on your journey."

The jicareros each gave their nineviery first, one by one. As always with Huichol it was very emotional. Since they were speaking in Huichol, I didn't understand most of what was said but know that a lot of the crying was for the stolen peyote plants that would never reproduce here again. When the jicareros were finished I went next, followed by Sage, Michael, and Carlos. Jesús went last and he was extremely emotional as well. During and after his nineviery, Jesús sprinkled drops of deer blood on and around the grandfather fire to bring forth the ancestor spirit to join us.

With our intentions and offerings properly placed, the hikuri began to hit our bloodstream and Jesús provided a few final suggestions to the tewaris. Included was a very important piece of advice; don't go outside the circle of light created by the grandfather fire for any reason. The light from grandfather provides many things and one of them is protection from malicious entities both in the physical realm and the spirit realm. Jesús explained that it is perfectly ordinary and fine to go pee or stand and stretch or whatever but all this can be done without leaving the light.

It's not necessary or desirable for this story to recount all that happened during the night. However, a brief summary reveals important situations and circumstances that were initiated by Jesús's listening to the ancestors and, therefore, resulted in us finding ourselves in the unlikely position of spending the night with three tewaris in Wirikuta eating peyote. From a physical perspective this is what happened:

Almost immediately after nineviery both Michael and Carlos succumbed to a gut-wrenching puking session. After they were finished and calmed down, they were given some more hikuri to make up for what they lost. This time they ate the hikuri with some orange slices and were able to keep it down. Sage did not get sick. During the first part of the night she dozed on and off, which is fairly typical the first time you eat hikuri. The rest of the night she spent peacefully gazing into the fire and listening to the songs of the marakáme.

Michael also dozed during the first few hours and then became very animated and alternately danced, sat down clapping, and stood staring into the darkness at the edge of the circle of light.

Carlos did not have a good trip. He spent most of the night pacing around or sitting and sobbing. At one point he wandered off and Rafael went to retrieve him at Jesús's instruction.

The jicareros sat peaceful in their dream trance but attentive to the tewaris. A few times throughout the night they ate more peyote and shared it with Jesús and me. They mostly took turns answering the chant verses of Jesús although sometimes they would all answer at once for a while. Except for a few short breaks, Jesús chant-sang the entire night.

Physically my night was very peaceful, and except for eating peyote and going to pee once, I sat in dream trance the whole night. Inwardly I was visited by the ancestors and at times they showed me what the tewaris were experiencing, especially Carlos. Just before dawn a spectacular nierika opened in front of me and I went on an amazing journey of flying like an eagle in a giant circle first over to Hauxamanaka, then down to Haramara, over Teakata, down to Xapawiyeme, and finally up and over Tuimayau and landing on the top of Reu'unar where I sat looking over Wirikuta until the little birds noticed me and started chirping in the predawn light. During my flight, I somehow happened to be flying over the sacred sites at the same time that various groups of Huichol pilgrims were visiting, and in each place the lead marakáme of the group looked up and saw me and waved me a greeting.

Once the sunlight threw back the darkness, Carlos excused himself and left the circle. Jesús encouraged the Americans to speak about their night if they wanted to. From what Sage described she had a full night of phosphine imagery, often described as visuals. These visuals of complex geometric patterns—often morphing into a kaleidoscope of colors, shapes, fractals, patterns, spirals, checkerboards, grids, webs, and funnels—are seen either drifting or radically crossing the visual field whether the eyes are open or closed. These visuals have been and still are recorded by Huichol artists in their weaving, embroidery, and their famous artwork of yarn and beads. For many Huichol it is considered a sacred obligation to record the images brought forth by the hikuri. The elaborate multicolored embroidery on Huichol clothing, especially those of the marakámes, are directly inspired by these visions.

It is interesting to note, and I have personally felt this many times, that these visual images feel extremely *important* when viewing them. They seem to be perfect geometric interpretations of your current state of mind at such a profound level that rational thought is left behind and is replaced with numinous understanding of abstract meaning. Instead of simply viewing these images on a movie screen of the mind, they somehow become alive with almost explosive quantities of energy.

Sage also went into the next phase of visual perception, which is quite different from the first. This perception occurs with eyes wide open to the environment (place). It begins grounded in the physical reality of where you are. Then perceivable edges and lines start to wriggle and twist. After a while, solid objects appear to blend or melt into one another. At this point the original objects are not recognizable or have transformed into something else entirely. Along with or aside from this, the perception of depth is radically altered. In some moments, objects in the background move forward and objects that are close up move back. Sage did not describe this but I have also experienced no depth at all. My visual field was flattened into a single sort of one-dimensional, all-encompassing image.

In Sage's case, I was pleased to hear her also describe that her experience was not limited to just her sense of sight. Sometimes people are so overwhelmed by the visuals of the peyote experience that they don't perceive what else is happening. Most commonly the hearing, or audio, sense is also affected in various ways. Sage described one very well. She heard a very simple musical tune or reverberation that played through her and replayed consistently until she snapped out of it, but afterward she still had clear memory of it. I have heard Huichol musicians describe this often as the way they learn their sacred tunes for the violin or guitar.

The last and most important thing Sage described was her message, which personally blew me away. She described coming down from the peyote as dawn was emerging and the little birds started chirping, singing, and flying about. During this time the little birdies gave her a task—to write a book.

The reason I was so blown away by this was that many years before, on my first trip to Wirikuta, I was given the same message by the little birdies. I had never even thought about writing a book before then and now you are reading my eighth published book! I held back from asking Sage if she received the message about what her book was to be about because my message didn't include that information and I spent over two years trying to figure it out.

All in all, Jesús described Sage's experience as superb for a gringo in Wirikuta. He said that her mood, which was shaped by her honesty in her confession, and her general positivity, opened the door for her to meet the peyote on terms that were nurturing for her. And not only that, she had received a task for her life, which is the main reason the Huichol matawámes come to Wirikuta. However, even after her positive experience with the hikuri, Sage admitted that she would not try it again and she would not suggest for her friends to try it either. She described feelings of not being in control, of walking on a thin and shaky line between holding on to who she was and letting go to total insanity. She felt that she got what she came for but it wasn't what she expected and she gave thanks to *whatever* that she was able to experience Wirikuta in the company of a Huichol marakáme and his companions.

Michael had an experience somewhat the same and yet totally different. He began, like most people, with the psychedelic light show— very similar to what Sage experienced. But then instead of continuing out like Sage did, he went in. For most of the night he performed a wrestling match with himself over the minutia of his life and it was an excruciating experience. He said he made a real attempt to connect to the marakáme's singing through dancing with it and moving with it and at times he felt like he did. He said there were moments when he felt like he somehow understood what Jesús was singing about even though he didn't know a single word of Huichol.

The only message that Michael said he received was that he was absolutely certain that people like him should not be eating peyote. He wholeheartedly agreed with Jesús that he was not prepared for this encounter, and even if he was in a clean state of mind he knew now that eating peyote should be left to those who have cultural experience with it and that those that don't have very little or no chance of receiving anything that will make a positive, long-lasting impression in their life. Michael was actually crying fairly hard when he finished by saying that he was profoundly grateful that the spirits of Wirikuta took it easy on him for his foolishness because he felt their true power and knew that they could have easily squashed him. He felt like they had pushed him to the edge of his limits, but they didn't shove him off the cliff.

Almost as soon as Michael was finished speaking, Carlos came back and he was out of breath. I doubt that he had heard anything that Sage or Michael had shared. While catching his breath, he hurriedly handed Michael a wad of bills. He told them he was giving their money back because it was wrong to take it and that he wouldn't be bringing any more people to the desert to eat peyote.

Sage asked him to explain what had happened to him. He said that there was too much to explain it all, that he may never be able to remember everything. He said that the spirits of Wirikuta had a party with his mind last night. But he was not a participant of the fiesta. He was the dance floor. He was the beer bottle. He was the urinal. They boogied on his mind, drank his energy, and then pissed him out onto the cold dark ground. And then, when he was totally spent they made him an offer. They convinced him that if he would leave the silly singing of the marakáme and the mirage of the firelight they would show him the *proper* way to conduct a ceremony with the peyote. That he would become a true marakáme and be wildly famous and wealthy.

Carlos said that he was totally convinced this was true so he walked off into the desert to find the kakayeri. But after leaving the light of the fire, he saw a dark, opaque cloud coming toward him and he knew it would destroy him. But he was frozen with fright and couldn't move. Just when the cloud was about to reach him he saw shadows on the ground in front of him made from a light source behind him. He turned to see a golden flame of light coming toward him that broke up the cloud and simultaneously picked him up and carried him back to his seat by the fire. The golden flame was the jicarero Rafael.

When Carlos was back sitting by the fire, he felt the safety of Grandfather and his companions. With this feeling inside him, he witnessed each of us as golden flames of fire instead of our purely human forms. But his coolio vision didn't last. It was opposed almost immediately by audible screams and visual movies in his mind. He heard the cries of the sacred plants as they were being dug up by narco-traffickers, the poachers of the holy land, the profit-blinded men of ignorance without shame. They were mocking him for his little enterprise of bringing people here and taking their money for three or four little tops of the cactus. The wicked men, oblivious to the ear-piercing screams of the peyotes, called out for him to join them if he was a real man.

Carlos recalled them coming to get him from behind in the darkness but then stopping at the light of the fire. But he could smell their putrid breath on his neck and their filthy odor swirling around him. He did not see himself as being the same as them, but they did, and that made him cringe. He could never be like them, he would never be like them, and right there he promised to Grandfather Fire to change his ways.

With that promise, the wicked men fled laughing and did not return. Carlos said he then fell into a sort of exhausted sleep but was still more or less awake mentally. He gazed into the fire and saw a man on a horse. The image began as barely perceptible—tiny and blurry. But the more he concentrated on it, the clearer it became and it seemed like the horseman was riding toward him from a great distance away. He felt that his life depended on the horseman reaching him so he concentrated with all his might on the man and his horse. They gradually became larger and larger, and the fire itself became larger and larger, until they finally filled the whole fire, which was by then the size of a full grown horse and rider.

Carlos desperately wanted to see the face of the rider but the flames were too bright. He didn't know what to do so he looked over to Jesús. Maybe Jesús could tell him what to do. But when he looked at Jesús he saw himself. The Jesús-Carlos person pointed to the rider and he saw clearly that the rider was also him!

Carlos said that he then looked more closely at himself/the rider and saw that he wore a badge and a gun and had official papers and stuff with him. In that moment he knew what he was. He was an official topil, a sheriff of the peyote desert, the exact men that he always avoided and tried to hide from.

So in the end, the three tewaris learned valuable lessons about the eating of peyote and two of them found life missions. Carlos said that they would go back and tell their friends not to come, that there would be no peyote ceremony. He thanked Jesús and promised that he would look into becoming a protector of Wirikuta. There were only a few men that patrolled the desert on horseback and they were not real police. They were just men who had horses and were hired to patrol the desert. They did not have special training like police officers but rather their job was to summon the police if and when necessary, more or less like security guards.

Happy to see the change in Carlos, I put my two cents in and told both him and Sage that the messages from Wirikuta can be challenging but not to give up if the going gets tough. I told them about my first message of writing a book and the struggles I had—the many times I gave up, the doubt of whether the message was real or not. I also told them that they did not need to consume peyote. This was particularly meant for Carlos. It always amazed me that I could simply *be* in that desert and feel the peyote. I have visited the peyote desert without harvesting or ingesting the cactus. It's kind of like when I visit the giant sequoias in California near my house. I don't eat them but I can certainly feel them and hear them and be in their same psychic space.

We left Carlos, Sage, and Michael as they were packing up their things to go back to Real de Catorce. On the walk back to the truck, I asked Jesús about what had just happened. He looked at me smugly and said, "Well, you did not see, but when I went ahead the first time to check who was having a fire in the sacred desert, I saw that some kakayeri were already around those kids. In that moment I was being tested by the ancestors. I think I passed. There will be a few less peyote-stealing kids around and maybe even one more protector."

Jesús and the jicareros were anxious to visit their favorite places in the desert where they had come on pilgrimages for the sacred hikuri in the past. We took the truck and drove for a while under the direction of Marcelino. When we were close to where he wanted to go, I found a fairly good place to park the truck out of view of the dirt road. We had to climb under an old barbed-wire fence that didn't look like it had been of any use for many years. Unfortunately these "ghost" fences are fairly common in Wirikuta from many years of the local Mexicans grazing goats.

Normally when I had been on pilgrimages to Wirikuta in the past, the pilgrims had a very rigorous set of rituals and traditions that had to be strictly adhered to in order for the hunt of the peyote to be successful. This is especially true when the whole group of cargo holders of a temple district come together to Wirikuta as part of their commitment to the community. On that type of pilgrimage where every single sacred place along the way is visited and honored according to the sacred traditions, all the taboos are strictly observed, the rituals are performed perfectly, and each cargo holder is performing their individual duties, the task and ultimate goal of finding and hunting down the peyote is much different from the context my four companions and I were currently experiencing.

Although our reverence for the sacred place was obvious in all of our thoughts and actions, we were not there to fulfill the obligations of the temple. We were there on a fact-finding mission, using all of our skills and talents to find out the current state of things in Wirikuta. But none of us were scientists. We weren't there to collect purely scientific data and make lists and charts. We were there to collect the status of the iyari of the hikuri.

With that said, it's important to note that all Huichol are extremely superstitious. They are like *super-super*-superstitious. So of course they had to do *something* in terms of ritual. It was my turn to laugh at Jesús and my Huichol companions as I looked at their somewhat confused faces. For myself, I had been to Wirikuta on occasions when I did not eat or collect any peyote. But I'm fairly certain that neither the jicareros nor Jesús ever had. And that was their quandary.

For once in their lives, they were not in Wirikuta for the same reasons they normally came there for and they were not expected or required to bring back peyote for the community. Whether or not any of them had planned on taking some peyote while they were in Wirikuta, I didn't know for sure, and it really wasn't any of my business. But for the moment at least, we were not there to harvest peyote—just to look for it and discover any other kind of evidence as to the current state of health of the hikuri.

After I had my laugh at (with) them and after some discussion, it was decided that at the very least our group should be blessed with sacred water and our faces painted with uxa from Tuimayau. The women of the pilgrimages are the ones to actually make the yellow paint after the men collect the yellow roots for them. Since we had only one woman with us, the duty fell to Maria to crush the root and make a paste for the face painting, which she expertly did.

Now painting with the uxa paste is not really like painting in the strict sense. It is usually applied in dots, always with a pointed *uru* (a thin wooden stick resembling a miniature arrow). The dots form patterns and designs on the face. I have always been fascinated by how or why specific designs end up on the pilgrims' faces, so I asked Maria as she was mixing up the paint.

According to her, and Jesús nodded yes many times while she explained, the experienced marakáme can see the "light" of people. Sometimes this is surrounding their body, sometimes it is inside. Sometimes it has colors of varying intensity pertaining to the health of the person. Sometimes they are like little lights flashing in the face. This last one is what is painted on the face in Wirikuta. It portrays both the current and future state of the person. This can be very complex to explain because the little lights can depict anything imaginable. But the painting of the face is also a signpost to the ancestors that the individual person is here to learn and experience and sacrifice. This face painting demonstrates clearly to ancestors that their children have arrived and want to visit with them. It is much easier for them to see us when we have put their paint and sacred designs on our faces.

With design-painted faces, each exhibiting our iyari, we began our exploration and what we found was not pretty. In many areas that historically produced large quantities of the cactus there were few or none to be found. Other areas still did seem to contain quite a bit, at least to me. However, practically everywhere we went that day there were signs of poachers—large areas of no peyote and small mounds of trash that poachers had left while camping for many days in the desert. The Huichol pilgrims don't leave trash in Wirikuta mainly out of respect but also because they don't bring anything with them that would become trash. They hardly ever eat on the pilgrimage and they certainly don't drink soda or beer or leave candy and potato chip wrappers on the ground.

Aside from the trash and lack of peyote in those areas, the other disturbing circumstance was the many holes we found all around. These holes indicated poachers taking whole plants for sale and not just the tops. If the peyote is harvested properly, with just the fleshy top taken but the root left intact, it will grow back naturally. Huichol never dig up plants. The taking of whole plants was the worst thing that could be happening for the future of the peyote.

Around nightfall, we once again noticed a fire lit not too far away from where we were. But this time we were deep into the desert and I got a bad feeling right away. It turns out that we had come across a group of poachers and the Huichol were not happy in the least. Jesús said that he had a vision of this group of men when we had our ceremony at Hauxamanaka and that they had been there for many days collecting peyote.

As we approached closer to the light of the fire, the distinct sound of mariachi music came to our ears and we halted. It seemed the people there were partying. So as before, Jesús gave us a signal to wait while he went and checked out the situation. Within minutes he was back and it was the first time I had seen him with a stern look on his face.

"It is as I saw in my vision. There are men and they have collected many large sacks of peyote. They are poachers* and we need to save those little deer."

"How many are there?" I asked.

"Two Americans and three Mexicans. They are not kids like the other ones and they are pretty drunk."

"Then it's unsafe to confront them," I said. "They are probably armed and dangerous. If they were here for spiritual reasons, they wouldn't be playing mariachi music and getting drunk."

We stood quietly thinking about what we should do, if anything, when suddenly one of their two trucks started up and its light went on.

"One or more of them are leaving," Jesús said hurriedly. "Rafael, you're the fastest. Run quickly and see if you can see anything in that pickup truck as it leaves. But don't let them see you!"

Quickly Rafael took off into the night crouching low as he ran. I was stunned at the sudden decisiveness of my friends but shouldn't have been so surprised knowing how sacred the peyote was to them.

The truck pulled away but from our vantage point we couldn't see Rafael. He returned a few minutes later. "The pickup truck had a web in the back instead of a gate so I could see inside. There were some things there. I think they were tools. But I didn't see any sacks or crates. I saw the backs of three heads so that means there are only two left there."

"They probably went to get more booze," Maria said with a frown.

"I say we go and get the hikuri they stole," Marcelino said excitedly while pulling out his machete.

Jesús thought for a moment and said, "No. We will not confront them with force. We must find another way."

---

*Peyote poachers come from many different countries but mostly the United States. If they successfully get the peyote out of Wirikuta, which in most cases they do, it is common for them to send the peyote to where they want it to go via Fed Ex or another carrier. No drug-detecting dogs are trained to sniff out peyote, so shipping it is much safer than trying to smuggle it across the border in their own vehicles, although sometimes they do that, too. Most of the peyote taken is used for recreational purposes, not religious reasons.

Standing there in silence for a few moments, Maria said eagerly, "I will do it."

"Do what?" I asked.

"I will distract them while you get the hikuri. You know as well as I do that I can run as fast as any of you and much faster than they can in this desert. Plus they are drunk. If they hear a woman's voice they will come looking for it."

"That's not a bad idea," I said. "I bet they'd come looking for you, too. But it's too dangerous. What if they catch you?"

"Let me do this, Grandfather!" Maria implored Jesús. "I will keep far enough away from them that they will never see me. I will lead them away with my voice and keep ahead of them making them run in circles until you are gone. They will *never* catch me!"

Jesús looked kindly at his granddaughter and said, "Very well. But I expect you to keep your word. Whatever happens, you must not be caught by them. If you are successful leading them away, we will grab the sacks and run for James's truck where we will be waiting for you."

I certainly didn't like the idea but the Huichol were set on getting that peyote from the poachers and I was fairly confident that they wouldn't catch Maria. I'm pretty sure I couldn't catch Maria in the desert of Wirikuta if she ran from me. And I wasn't drunk.

So the four of us men snuck closer while Maria made a wider birth to get to the opposite side of them from where my truck was parked. As we inched forward we could clearly see the two men sitting by the fire. But the music also became louder the closer we got. One thing we hadn't thought of was how close Maria would need to be in order for them to hear her over the music but not be seen.

A few excruciating minutes later we heard Maria scream from the distance, and it was way loud enough for the poachers to hear. They both jumped up and looked toward the sound of the woman's scream. They quickly conversed, probably asking each other about what they had just heard. A few moments went by and Maria screamed again.

Well, that was all it took for the men, and they quickly ran off in

search of the screaming. This was our chance and we took it. With light-
ning speed we ran into the camp and each shouldered two big burlap
sacks filled with peyote. There was only one left and I quickly pondered
what the Huichol would do. But I shouldn't have wondered. These were
farm people and strong as oxen. Especially Rafael, who somehow managed to get a third sack on his shoulders.

We took off running toward the truck and I have to admit that
even though what we were doing was dangerous, I was having a really
good time. My adrenaline was pumping and I barely noticed the heavy
sacks on my shoulders as I ran. We made it back to the truck in record
time and began loading the sacks in the truck, but they wouldn't all fit
with room for us to sit. Not surprisingly the Huichol, accustomed their
whole lives to loading mules and horses, quickly tied the two remaining
sacks to the roof.

Only a few nervous minutes passed and Maria was back with us
and we all jumped in the truck headed in the opposite direction of the
poachers. The Huichol knew the terrain in Wirikuta much better than
the poachers and we had a head start so I didn't even see any lights following us. Jesús said that we would go near to the tiny town of Wadley,
just outside the peyote desert, where he had some Mexican friends that
were friendly to the Huichol.

Our drive through the desert was uneventful except for all the
laughing and blowing of bull horns by the Huichol. We arrived at the
small shack of a house that belonged to Jesús's friend and he went inside.
Within a few minutes he came back out and said that we could stash
the peyote in his friend's barn, which we did, and after Jesús blessed the
peyote sacks with deer blood and holy water we were off again.

Jesús didn't want to spend the night in Wadley and announced that
at first light we would climb the sacred mountain of Reu'unar and, on the
way, visit the cave of Pariteká where the Father Sun first emerged. We had
a fairly short drive to get to the base of the mountain where we camped
out for the night. I was extremely tired and slept most of the night curled
up by the fire while the Huichol conversed about all that had happened.

In the morning, the Huichol were all excited about the hike to the top of Reu'unar, their most sacred place in the East. With the truck stowed in what seemed like a safe place, we began our trek. It wasn't too long, maybe an hour or so when we hit a dry wash that went straight up the mountain. The intensity of the Huichol grew with each step and soon we were at the small cave of Pariteká. Many candles were lit and prayer arrows made and left in the sacred place of the Father Sun.

We hiked up another couple hours until we hit the top and came upon the rirriki of Reu'unar, one of the five main sacred sites in Huichol cosmology. Due to the growing number of tourists coming to Real de Catorce, which was close by, the rirriki at this site was built extra strong. After many years of tourists stealing offerings and artifacts from the open rirriki, the Union of Jicareros de Jalisco constructed a permanent stone structure with a solid roof and door that was locked. I was actually part of the fund-raising efforts to construct the rirriki and had been there twice before.

The rirriki actually has a Huichol doorkeeper who temporarily lives at the sacred site, and as a tewari I was obliged to pay 20 pesos (less than two U.S. dollars) to be there, which I did. The ceremony that Jesús and my friends performed that day was very intense and had a very different feeling since there was no fire and it was daytime. In this case the Father Sun was the light and nierika, instead of the Grandfather Fire. Jesús suggested that I allow the light and energy of the Father Sun on the top of this sacred mountain to bathe my essence in the feelings of la gloria.

Many offerings were made and blessed with deer blood and water from the five directions. After the blessings and prayers, the offerings were placed in the rirriki, including the deer antlers that Maria was carrying. She spent a long time in the rirriki thanking the spirit of the exceptional ancestor and she proved that she was true to her word by bringing part of his essence to this sacred site where he may be reincarnated again and roam the holy peyote desert.

The Chief

"Vision from the sacred mountain has directed me that James and I need to go across the border and see what is currently happening with the hikuri in Texas," Jesús announced to the group.

"First I will walk to Real de Catorce and report on the poachers. Then I will go to Matehuala and take a bus to Monterrey where I have friends. From there I will find a way to Rio Grande City [Texas], crossing into the United States over the Puente Camargo [Camargo Bridge]. We will meet again in either Rio Grande City or farther north in Mirando City," Jesús said forcefully to me.

Jesús immediately saw my look of trepidation at what seemed to me an overly ambitious and destined-to-fail excursion into the United States for this Huichol holy man. But once again I was surprised, as I have been throughout my many years dealing with the Huichol, at his resourcefulness and experience. "I have many friends in Texas and Arizona," he added with a smile.

He pretty much alleviated my concerns by producing a folder-type wallet from his moral. "I have a passport, visa, and all necessary documents, including an open-ended invitation from Native American Church officials to participate and officiate in church functions."

Jesús smiled at me proudly and let me examine his documents, which all seemed well in order. I was surprised to see on his passport that he had visited the United States many times before and was happy to see his letter from the NAC. Since the tragedy of September 11 and increased security at the borders, it is extremely difficult for a poor indigenous person to cross the border, even with a valid passport. For an indigenous person to obtain a visitor's visa it is required to show evidence of funds sufficient for travel and expenses, and demonstrate social and economic ties to Mexico that will compel return at the end of their stay. The thinking of the government is that when someone like Jesús, an indigenous person with little money, enters the United States he will likely try to stay illegally. Proof of what they are going to do, why they are requesting entry, where they will stay, and bona fide letters from a legitimate U.S. institution or company (such as a church, art gallery, or university) are standard requirements. Surprisingly Jesús had it all.

But in that moment I was supremely reluctant to leave Jesús to make this journey without me and had doubts I would actually find him when I got to Texas. I had never even been to Texas. Plus, I still had to travel all the way back to the Sierra with the Huichol and sacks filled with peyote. Since he was the leader of our group, I much preferred that he join me on the trip back to the Sierra and then we travel together to the United States. But he was adamant, stating he needed to go right away and added that he thought it would be a good experience for me to travel back to the Sierra with our group and that they would be supremely grateful for the ride.

Desperate to change his mind, a thought came to me, "Jesús, don't you need to go back now, even for a short while? What about your duties as judge?"

He waved his hand at me, "My cargo was over in January and the staff has been passed to the new judge. Most importantly I have completed my obligations and tied up all the loose ends. The new juez will do a fine job. James, it is settled, I am going to Texas, you are going back to the Sierra to deliver the jicareros, and we will meet up in Texas when you arrive."

The other Huichol, my friends and now *companeros,* were clandes-tinely listening so when I headed toward them after saying goodbye to Jesús they immediately grabbed all their things and jumped into the truck. Maria, who would now be riding with me in the front of the truck, slapped me on the back and goodheartedly assured me I was doing the right thing. "Jesús will be fine, he is a marakáme. *We* need to get all this peyote to the Sierra. You are the official gringo chauffer! Drive on, brother!"

As I climbed into the driver's seat, I saw Jesús with his muvieris out and waving them in the air and while chanting prayers he touched them to the wheels and motor of the truck in blessing us for a safe trip. I pulled away with tears in my eyes at leaving him, but for the next two days everything went according to plan, which is fairly unusual while travel-ing through rural Mexico. I arrived at the town of Huejuquilla without incident and with a group of very happy and appreciative Huichol.

Now that I was so close to the Huichol homeland, I was tempted to go all the way back with them. I was curious as to what would happen when they arrived with their stories and sacks of hikuri. But I decided, with the help of my companeros, that it was best for me to find and help Jesús on his mission in the United States. So late the next day, I was crossing into the United States over the Rio Grande River via the Roma-Ciudad Miguel Alemán International Bridge.

The border crossing was hectic, and the officials at the border took their time rummaging through my truck while glaring at me. I really didn't care about their scrutiny; they had no idea what I had just been through. My only thought was catching up with Jesús but I hadn't heard from him. We agreed before I left him that one of his friends would contact me via my cell phone and instruct me as to where he was. With no other choice, I decided to drive the half hour to Rio Grande City.

Having never been to Texas and knowing nothing about Rio Grande City, I asked for information at a *Welcome to Texas* store and tourist office situated on the highway just across the border. Turns out Rio Grande City is the county seat of Starr, not a big place, with a population of around thirteen thousand. Historically it was an important trade route between Mexico and the United States via the many steamboats that operated on the Rio Grande.

Without a plan, I drove around town for a while until I spotted an unusual shrine to the Virgin Mary across the street from the courthouse. The shrine was built to resemble a hillside and constructed of rock and petrified wood. It appeared to be three or four stories high with cave-like openings, the biggest cave holding a giant statue of Mary. While driving by, I caught my breath at the sight of a man in Huichol clothing kneeling in front of the statue of Mary. Quickly I parked the truck and walked over to the man. It was Jesús. He had some of his muvieris in hand and appeared to be sobbing while praying when I found him.

I gently touched his shoulder, and he looked up at me with tear-filled eyes. "It is as I expected here," he said. "The landowners have fenced off even more land, so the few areas where one can collect the medicine have been decimated by too much harvesting. There is not enough medicine* available for all the people. We must find answers to this problem. I have come to speak to the Mothers here at this shrine."

Jesús stood and put away his muvieris. With an air of compassion and devotion he explained, "When I was younger I traveled to Europe to show my artwork in galleries and to sell them. One time I visited France and since my sponsors for the trip were Catholic they took me to the Sanctuary of Our Lady of Lourdes. That place is incredible. There are many churches and hundreds of priests, all because of the visions of a young girl in the 1800s. This girl was looking into a small cave [grotto] where some roses were growing outside and she saw visions of a young woman. The young woman told her to the drink the water from the sacred spring that flowed from the cave and also told her to build a church. When word of this spread, many people came from all around and they were healed by the waters. The first church was built in honor of these miracles.

---

*The term *medicine* is commonly used by tribes in the United States when talking about peyote.

"But of course the Catholics took the girl's visions and interpreted them for themselves. They figured that it had to be visions of the Virgin Mary and had a sculptor make a statue to put in the cave for all to see and pray upon. But I was there! I felt the waters and had my own visions. The little girl saw what I saw and the vision has little to do with Catholic dogma. These visions and the waters are for everyone. They are the Mothers of creation speaking to us. I have been to Catholic mass hundreds of times in my life and I'm still not sure that the Virgin Mary ever even existed! But I know the Mothers exist. I see them every day, I drink and eat of them every day.

"I come to this giant shrine, made as a replica of the shrine in France, because the priest who built it with his bare hands, gathering rocks from all around these hills, must have felt the Mothers when he visited the shrine in France and wanted to bring those feelings here. He also must have felt the spirit of the hikuri, which grew in much abundance here when this shrine was built many decades ago. This shrine contains the bones of this land, which is blessed by the sacred hikuri. It is a place of much power and today I come seeking answers to important questions and to ask the Mothers for guidance. I have received many instructions from the Mothers, but first tell me about your trip."

I told Jesús that the trip back to the Sierra went without a hitch and I could tell he was pleased. But I wanted to know what had happened to him and what he planned on doing. "Yes, yes," he said with a laugh while we walked over to my truck. He actually petted the truck as if it were a dog or cat and added, "Very nice and very handy this truck you have. It is powered by Grandfather Fire and flies like *Welika* [Sacred Royal Eagle]. We must go now to Mirando City and, along the way, visit with the hikuri. But first let's get some food in us and I will tell you what you want to know."

We stopped to eat at a small Mexican restaurant, of which there were many in Rio Grande City since it has a very large Mexican-American population. During our meal Jesús was very animated, and I learned a lot about the situation regarding the medicine in Texas.

"There are good and bad things happening here," Jesús began. "On the one hand you have these ranchers putting up giant fences all around their land to keep people out and keep their livestock in, or in some cases game animals like deer inside for private hunting. They make a lot of money by charging people to hunt on their land and they even have guards that patrol in jeeps and on motorcycles. For the medicine, for the hikuri, this is actually a good thing because, knowing it or not, the ranchers are protecting it from poaching and farming. But some ranchers are also destroying the medicine by root plowing fields to grow food for their cattle. This kills all the medicine. The ranchers don't care at all about the medicine so they are not likely to stop. They simply see no reason to care about the sacred cactus because it has no value to them.

"Right now the problem that concerns me the most is that while a good portion of the medicine is being inadvertently protected by these fences, there is not enough medicine for the people. The roadmen of the Native American Church, the leaders of the peyote ceremonies, need the sacrament for the people. It cures them of the alcohol, and it relieves them from the depression of life on the reservations as it puts them in direct contact with the Mothers and Fathers. This contact revives their sacred connection to the divine, to the land, to their family, and their tribe."

"Living with the Huichol, I have seen the deep connection between your people and the peyote, the corn, the land, the deer, and the ceremonies that continue the balance, the sacred dance, of human activity and the greater forces that control the world," I replied.

Jesús shook his head emphatically while biting his torta. "We must find a way to balance this delicate relationship here between the dwindling populations of the medicine with the increase in consumption. Some have suggested bringing the medicine from Mexico where it is more abundant but I don't see that as a solution at this time. As you have plainly seen, Wirikuta has its own problems. Plus the governments of both Mexico and the United States will not allow it or even bring it up for discussion."

"That's true," I added. "For whatever reasons, in their minds they consider the medicine a dangerous drug. But yet they consider alcohol and tobacco okay and collect taxes on them, all the while also endorsing the legal sale of all kinds of antidepressants, antianxiety drugs, and most recently drugs for what is being called attention deficit hyperactivity disorder in children, all of which make billions of dollars for the pharmaceutical companies."

"All those people taking those pitiful drugs, especially the kids, need to get their asses into the woods for a while, go on a vision quest and find out what the Mothers and Fathers want them to do with their life. Then they won't be all depressed and stressed out," Jesús commented sternly.

Finishing our meal, Jesús said, "I saw an authentic Collins machete yesterday in a store near here, it's older than I am but unlike me it's in perfect condition. I want you to buy it for me. And buy me a new file to sharpen it with. We need some new things to go along with these new thoughts. This machete is old, but it was crafted in a time when things were made to last and it is a perfect symbol for the hikuri to see that we are serious."

I must say Jesús's new machete was cool, and after we (I) purchased it, we headed up the road to Mirando City. A sign on the road told me we were on FM-3167, which basically told me we were headed into the boonies. I had learned earlier from the map I got at the information stop that farm-to-market (FM) and ranch-to-market (RM) roads were typically two-lane paved roads built and maintained by the Texas Department of Transportation to serve as access to rural communities.

After about an hour, we had turned onto 649 and Jesús exclaimed, "Turn here!" and pointed to small dirt road off to our left. "I feel the calling of the hikuri."

A mile or two down the one-lane dirt road, Jesús told me to park and he hurriedly exited the vehicle carrying his new machete and one of his morals. To my dismay he rapidly walked into the darkness of the desert chaparral.

"Wait up," I said into the pitch black darkness but Jesús didn't slow and it wasn't until after several minutes of scrambling through the thorny brush that I found him stopped in front of a large fence.

"We must find a way in," he said earnestly. "Come on this way."

"Wait!" I replied. "Are we going to hunt peyote?"

He stopped for just a second and said, "Just one. We are answering the call of a chief—an ancestor hikuri."

Just then he jumped down into an *arroyo* (an eroded gulley) and showed me that we could slide under the fence. I wasn't very comfortable trespassing but I followed Jesús under the fence and for about another half mile, when he stopped and pointed. "Up there on the side of that hill," he said excitedly.

It was very dark in the middle of the desert chaparral filled with scrub bushes and snakes. The tops of peyote plants grow level with the ground and usually under a bush or even under rocks so they are not easy to find even in the daylight. Trying to find the medicine in these conditions was not very likely. Or so I thought. For the Huichol medicine man this proved not to be a problem. The hill he pointed to was not much more than a slight rise in the terrain, but I did feel the ground become rockier as we went up.

Jesús suddenly stopped, bent low under a bush, and with a loud "Ha-ha!" he knelt on the ground.

"I knew the Chief was here!" He exclaimed. "He was calling me and wants to help us. He wants to help the ancestors, his brothers and sisters, and the people. This is his destiny, this is why the creator and the blue deer put him here. This is the reason for his life. He is happy we have come!"

For the next twenty minutes or so Jesús spoke in Huichol to the large (maybe five inches in diameter) Chief peyote, and quite frankly I have no idea what he said but there was both weeping and laughing in his conversation. He then took out his new machete and with his muvieris he blessed it by dribbling deer blood and sacred water onto it. With that done, he dug a little bit of soil away from around the Chief and very carefully sliced off the head, being sure to leave the root intact for future regeneration. Incredibly, when he did that I could swear that I saw some sort of colorful sparks or energy crystals fly from his machete.

Jesús carefully placed the head of the Chief inside his takwatsi. With his muvieris in hand he lovingly blessed the root and the ground around it with sacred water and deer blood. He rose and facing the four directions in turn shouted thanks to the sacred places and the ancestor deities that ruled them. For the fifth direction, the Center, he stood me close to the root and blessed me with holy water and deer blood.

"We must leave here now, it is not safe for us to linger here. We will drive farther toward Mirando and spend the night in Los Ojuelos," Jesús explained.

Without talking we made our way back to the truck and again began traveling north on 649. While we were riding along, Jesús told me that the only place in the United States where hikuri grows naturally is a small belt of land that runs from Rio Grande City (where I found him) north to just outside Mirando City. This belt is only about ninety miles long and less than twenty miles wide. The two-lane road on which we were now traveling runs up through pretty much the middle of this belt.

When we were a few miles from Mirando City, he told me to slow down. We gradually came to a group of dilapidated buildings on the sides of the road, the remnants of a small town, which gave me the distinct feeling of a ghost town. He instructed me to turn onto a small dirt road and park behind the shell of an old building.

"I know the owner of this land," he said. "We should be safe here. We will pass the night here in the company of Grandfather Fire to receive instructions on what to do next."

Without chitchat we grabbed a few of our belongings and Jesús led us a short distance to an old fire pit dug into the ground and circled with a ring of stones. For the next half hour we collected brush and brought it back for the fire.

Jesús lit the fire and got comfortably seated, as did I. He then methodically brought forth from one of his morals a jar that I was surprised to see, and also a gourd bowl that I immediately recognized. With practiced precision he filled the gourd with water, shook some of the contents of the jar into the gourd and stirred it rapidly with one of his muvieris until the mixture created a foamy beverage that he drank from and then passed to me.

With a glint of fire reflecting in his eyes, he casually explained that before we left the Easter ceremony in Santa Catarina he spoke to the old kawitéro and his wife and they gave him my jar of hikuri powder for safekeeping and for our journey. I had taken it back to them before I left, as I was not safe carrying it out of the Sierra.

With a smile he added, "I hid it in my belt [a Huichol sash with yarn tassels] when I crossed the border. I have no right or desire to consume hikuri from this place. I have taken a chief but that I will gift to one of the roadmen we will meet. We need the Chief as our guide but we will not ingest this ancestor. I will only take into my body the spirit of the hikuri that comes from Wirikuta, unless I am told otherwise."

Passing the gourd between us, we drank until it was empty and then without delay Jesús began his oration.

"We sit now in a very important place in the history of hikuri in your country. This little old town is called Los Ojuelos. It means "bright and lovely eyes" in Spanish. It was given that name because of the springs of water that flow from the ground near here. The water is supremely sacred here in the desert. The Natives who lived here guarded it fiercely and chased many gringos off this land when they tried to take it. But I also believe it was named thusly because of the lovely eyes of the hikuri. They could have named it *los manantiales,* or other names more appropriate for the words *springs of water.*

"In any case, we are here because this is a seat of power. Not in the logical, rational, sense. There is no economy here, there is no hustling-bustling of city life and politics. As you can see it is basically deserted. Here there is only desert and many dreams that have gone by. *But,* here, for eyes that can see, it is a most sacred place. A woman that I knew and held in high esteem once lived here. She was a peyotera [collector

and seller of peyote]. Her father before her and her husband were peyoteros too. People would come great distances to buy from them and she
would also send the medicine to roadmen from all over by mailing it.
But I'm getting ahead of myself now. There are others that you may
meet tomorrow and in the future that can tell you and I more of the
recent history of the hikuri and the NAC in your country. I can tell you
what I know, what I remember of my talks with the roadmen, but first
tell me of what you know. You said you have never been to Texas and
the hikuri fields here."

"That's true," I replied. "I'm kind of embarrassed to say it, but until
only a few years ago I didn't even know that hikuri grew outside of
Wirikuta—and especially not in the United States. I had heard about
the Native American Church but I lived in Pennsylvania and had no
contact with them. It wasn't until I moved to Arizona and one of my
Huichol friends from Las Latas came to visit me that I learned more.
He was the one who introduced me to the NAC because like you he
has an open invitation to participate in NAC ceremonies and has a letter from them. He introduced me to a man living outside of Tucson
that "rescues" small peyotes from the farmers here in Texas who harvest them too young and small. He replants them and has thousands
in the back of his house. I was also introduced to a Navajo roadman
in Arizona and I was invited once to a teepee ceremony near Window
Rock. But this ceremony with the hikuri was so different from my experiences with your people, and it was so rigid compared to your ceremonies that I haven't done another one."

"Yes, depending on the roadman in charge, the all-night teepee ceremony can be very strict. We can talk more of that later."

"Tell me, Jesús," I asked. "How do you know so much of the history
of this place?"

With a sigh he replied, "Like I said before, I have been coming
here for many years and I have very knowledgeable friends that I have
sat with for many long nights having discussions. This area is a seat of
power not only because it is where the medicine grows but also because

of all the different people that come here. Chiefs and roadmen from some fifty or more tribes come here for the medicine to bring back to the people. Sometimes they stay for many days, there are meetings and ceremonies and much information is shared. But enough about me. Tonight, in this spirit of sharing I will give you a brief history lesson so you will know better. And also it is good for me to repeat these things so I do not forget.

"There have been many Native tribes living and passing through this area throughout history. The most important in this tale of the medicine were the Caohuiltecan Carrizo, who some people called the Barefoot Indians because they wore only sandals, just like my people still do. Also there were the Lipan Apache who later in the early 1800s formed alliance with the Carrizo. It is said that the Carrizo who once inhabited this region are directly responsible for the spread of the medicine in the United States. The Carrizo taught the Apache, and contact with the Carrizo brought the medicine to the Kiowa, the Comanche, and the Mescaleros. Also north of here in Texas were the Caddo, the Karankawa, and the Tonkawa, all familiar with the medicine.

"Unfortunately for the Carrizo, most if not all of them died here in Texas. This was a very dangerous place for many reasons and for a time no Indians were even allowed to live here. Spain lost control to Mexico, Mexico had its internal revolutions, and the United States was still fighting for control of Texas. But the seeds the Carrizo helped to plant grew and traveled with other tribes. Some of the Lipan Apache moved to New Mexico and others went to the reservations in Oklahoma. Knowledge of the medicine spread quickly when other tribes were also sent to Oklahoma. The Kiowa and the Comanche, among many other tribes of the Plains, were forced to sign treaties giving up their lands, their weapons, their traditional way of life and sustenance. All ended up on reservations in Oklahoma in the late 1800s and were put in close vicinity to the eastern tribes that were already relocated there, including the Five Civilized Tribes: the Creek, the Seminole, the Cherokee, the Choctaw, and the Chickasaw, among others.

"During this bloody time period of rounding up the 'wild Indians' it was extremely dangerous for any Indians to travel or be around the medicine here in Texas. But a few of the brave or maybe crazy ones could not be kept living on the reservation and secretly traveled from Oklahoma down here to Texas and back, always on the run from the Texas Rangers and the U.S. Army. A couple of these guys were Lipan Apache who had ancestors in these parts. They would come down right here in Los Ojuelos to buy the medicine from the first peyoteros. So anyway, they are given credit for keeping the spirit of the medicine alive among the tribes living on the reservations in Oklahoma, where a new sort of religion was about to be born.

"In the late 1800s railroad lines were completed between Texas and near to the reservations in Oklahoma, and a lot of medicine began to be available to the Indians because of that. Around that same time, another important thing was happening. Indians were being sent to the Carlisle Indian School in Pennsylvania to learn how to be 'white men.' They were taught English, Christianity, farming, and so on. This was important to the further spread of the medicine because now the 'educated' Indians spoke a common language whereas earlier many of them couldn't speak to each other. Even though many tribes were forced to live close together in Oklahoma, their native tongues were different.

"Their education in Christianity also seeped into the peyote ceremonies, as can still be seen today. It was and still is common for a roadman to practice three forms of spirituality all at once: traditional tribal ceremony [shamanism], peyote ceremony, and Christianity.

"Although the word is that he never claimed to be Christian, one of the first and most famous men of the medicine in Oklahoma was Quanah Parker, leader of the Comanche. Quanah sent his kids to the Carlisle Indian School because he knew the importance of education and learning English. He did business with white cattle ranchers and spoke highly of those whites who held the morals and values of Christians. As a Comanche chief, businessman, and leader of the peyote ceremony he often traveled to Washington and helped to retain the use of peyote when the government agencies wanted to squash it. The peyote ceremony used by Parker is called the half-moon ceremony and is still used today."

Jesús whipped us up another gourd full of medicine and after we drank and relieved ourselves in the bushes he continued, "Another famous man of the medicine was the Delaware-Caddo man, John Wilson. The story goes that together with his wife, he went out into the country and found a peaceful, quiet place in nature to gather information and direction from the peyote. For a few weeks, he lived in seclusion eating the peyote and received the call to be a roadman. He supposedly received guidance to deliver to the people a new form of ceremony, although in many ways it is the same as Parker's. Wilson's ceremony became known as the big moon and later the cross-fire ceremony—the main differences being the size of the altar and the addition of more Christian symbolism and vocabulary. Wilson's ceremony was also more complex.

"It is said that although many people began following "the Wilson way," others were not happy with the additional Christian elements and that Wilson didn't incorporate the ancient tribal mythology as Parker did. Wilson apparently didn't care because he said that he was given the ceremony directly from the peyote and that was all that mattered. Both the half-moon and cross-fire ceremonies are still used today; some people participate in both depending upon which is available and which roadman is available.

"Wilson also claimed that the peyote taught him how to make the sacred items of the ceremony: the water drum and drum stick, the feathered fan, the prayer stick, and the gourd rattle. He was also told how the people should dress, how to act, and the special duties of the officers of the ceremony. Wilson also received over two hundred peyote songs, many of which are still sung today."

Jesús stopped talking and for a long while we both stared into the fire and periodically fed the grandfather. With the sacred cactus flowing through my veins, visions and memories of my one tepee-style ceremony with the Navajos and my many occasions with peyote in Huichol ceremonies and pilgrimages entered my mind. It was a multicolored whirlwind of experiences, feelings, and deep emotions, some ecstatically beautiful and others deathly scary.

Sometime later, Jesús mixed another batch of medicine and after we both drank he began again.

"The main reason I am here now, in this seat of power, is because the use of the medicine has spread far from its homeland and also far from its adopted homeland in Oklahoma and is now in danger. The Wilson big-moon way is now often called the cross-fire way and the Comanche half-moon way is called the tepee way. The two 'ways' still retain most of their similarities: sitting around the sacred fire in a circle, the altar made of dirt or sand in the shape of a half-moon or a bigger moon, the chief peyote resting in the center of the moon, four officials that conduct the ceremony, everyone sitting basically all night in prayer and drumming and singing, feather fans and gourd rattles, no alcohol, and the sense of being in the presence of a higher power and feelings of kinship and healing within the group.

"The Wilson cross-fire way is still more Christian and complex, sometimes even using the Bible. The tepee way seems to have more Christian symbolism incorporated now but is still the more conservative of the two. Both are good medicine for the people. My concern now is how they have spread.

"The Navajo nation is now more than 300,000 souls in Arizona, New Mexico, and Utah, and they buy at least half of all the peyote available. But aside from the Oklahoma tribes and the Navajo, there are tribes in California, Washington, Montana, Idaho, Nevada, Colorado, Wyoming, North and South Dakota, Nebraska, Kansas, Iowa, Wisconsin, Minnesota, and maybe more that want the medicine. And let's not forget the Canadian tribes, too. This tiny little area of desert where we now sit cannot possibly sustain all these people— especially with ranchers now prohibiting the peyoteros from harvesting on most of the land.

Jesús carefully brought out the Chief peyote we had collected and placed it between him and the fire. "Please, James," he said. "Feed the grandfather some and I am going to dream with the Grandfather and this Chief until the sun comes up."

I built up the fire as Jesús pulled a blanket close around himself and put his chin to his chest and went off to dreamland. I did the same.

The next thing I remember is waking up to the sound of barking dogs. The sun had not yet risen but it was twilight and looking around me I could make out at least five dogs surrounding us. The dogs seemed to be trained to bark before biting, as if signaling their owner of intruders. Jesús and I, still wrapped in our blankets, sat perfectly still and in a few moments we were joined by two men on all-terrain vehicles.

The younger of the two got off his four-wheeler and grabbed his rifle from the front rack. Cocking a shell into the chamber, he walked over to Jesús. He seemed to be of Mexican blood, in his twenties, tall and lanky, and weathered from life on the desert ranch.

"Just what the hell are you doing here," he said gruffly.

Jesús didn't move or answer so not knowing what else to do, I interjected. "There's no need for your guns and dogs, we were simply passing the night here and were getting ready to leave."

"Y'all come here after peyote, I reckon. I'm sick of you hippie freaks. This here is *private* property."

Jesús slowly reached for his machete. His move received two raised rifles at him.

In his best Spanish, Jesús said, "I know the owners of this land; I have permission to be here."

"Well, the owner ain't here right now, is he?" The ranch hand replied rather nastily. "I'm the boss here and I say y'all are trespassing. Keep your hands where I can see them, no funny stuff or you'll get a bullet and then be dog food."

Quickly and efficiently he searched our bags and while the other man held us at gunpoint from his four-wheeler, he searched my truck, then came back to us obviously frustrated at finding nothing that he was looking for. He put the barrel of his gun to Jesús's chest.

Jesús slowly stood up and his blanket fell away.

"Well, looky here," the young man said. "You dressed for the circus or what?"

Jesús's finely embroidered clothes shone brightly in the rising sunlight, the colorful images of flowers, deer, and peyote adorned him.

"That guy is a Huichol," the older man said. "Leave 'im be, I doubt he's doin' nothin' wrong. I think I remember him."

Obviously annoyed, the younger man walked over to me and smacked me in the face with the butt of his rifle.

"Get the hell out of here and don't ever let me see you again," he said as I staggered to my feet.

I was pretty close in my mind to retaliating. As a kid I had been in many fights, and I wasn't afraid of this bully. But as I was brushing myself off upon standing, I glanced at Jesús's moral and the Chief, which the ranch hand somehow didn't find. The Chief spoke to me and told me that we were destined to have met these guys. They, and those like them, were one of the reasons we were here. The Chief told me we were there to learn and not to fight.

Jesús smiled at me and I immediately knew he had heard the same words from the Chief. We quickly grabbed our things and left in the truck.

Medicine Lodge

My head ached on the short drive to Mirando City but at least I wasn't bleeding. Jesús instructed me to drive up a dirt road just outside of town. We passed under a wrought-iron gateway with the emblem of the Native American Church and parked next to a large building. Immediately a number of men came out of the brick structure.

We were greeted warmly by all the men of various ages, who were all dressed alike in jeans, cowboy boots, buttoned-down shirts and cowboy-style hats. The tallest man, who seemed to be in charge, hugged Jesús with reverence and then introduced himself to me. His name was Marcelino; he was a very big man with strong hands and a broad smile. It occurred to me that he had wisdom gained by passing through many struggles and hardships, but he had made it through and now possessed humor in the face of difficulty.

Marcelino put his hands on my bruised face and with a chuckle asked us inside to tell them our story. Surprisingly, when we entered I was immediately struck by the light of a fire built in a shallow pit in the center of the floor. I was not expecting to see the dirt floor, the fire, and the half-moon altar built between the fire and the West wall. Looking up I saw a round copper structure built into heavy wooden beams in the roof. This was where the smoke from the fire exited so it was not very smoky inside the building. But there was enough smoke to make the sunlight coming through small windows located in the center of each wall cast surreal beams of light, kind of like the sun piercing through clouds in majestic rays.

The thought came to me that the place felt very similar to the Huichol kalliway temple—related in feeling and design. On the opposite side of the building from the altar were some chairs in a circle and we all sat down. For the next few minutes we spoke about our incident with the ranchers. The men seated around me were stern as I recounted the story.

"Those guys were doing their jobs; they are not friendly toward us either," Marcelino said gruffly. "But now you are among friends. We are honored by the gift of the Huichol holy man coming to see us, and you, James, for accompanying him."

Marcelino and Jesús met eyes. After a few moments Marcelino spoke again. "I can see we have other things to discuss. Important things. Tell us, Jesús, what brings you to us today."

Jesús carefully brought out the Chief and set him on the dirt floor in the center of our circle. "I am here on behalf of the hikuri. Told very directly to speak to my Northern brothers in this time of crisis, I come here to suggest we have a peyote ceremony and hear what this Chief has to say."

Marcelino gazed over to the fire and then stared intently at the Chief for a long while. He then looked at each man in the circle and responded, "This Chief comes from this land, he has much to say. We will make ceremony and listen. He will guide us; he will sing his songs through us. Jesús will be our roadman."

"No," Jesús replied. "The Chief told me last night we need a roadman from the North. I would very much like to take the position of sponsor for the ceremony, James to be fire man, Marcelino to be cedar man."

"Those positions are determined by the roadman. And it is unusual to have a fire man who is not a church member," replied Marcelino.

Jesús stood and addressed Marcelino. "James carries the spirit of the medicine within him, he has passed through many ceremonies and hardships to be here. More than five times he has been to Wirikuta and has a direct connection with the Grandfather Fire."

One of the elder men laughed out loud and I thought it was going to be a problem. But it was just the opposite. Still laughing he said, "So he's a gringo shaman."

All the men laughed and a lighter mood filled the atmosphere. I thought they were going to pick on me but instead each man in turn stood, took off his hat, and shook my hand profusely.

With a beaming smile, Jesús sat back down. Marcelino sat back comfortably in his chair, stretched his legs out in front of him, and lit a cigarette. This was a sign that all was okay and most of the other men also began to smoke.

"Red Cloud," one of the men suddenly said. "I saw him yesterday at the market, he's visiting from Wyoming. He would be the perfect road-man for this. I have been in ceremony with him, he's an Arapaho chief and experienced roadman."

Marcelino looked to Jesús. Jesús slapped my leg and then stood addressing the group. "Settled. I know Red Cloud, too. He's also been to Wirikuta. Let's get him before he goes back home."

Marcelino gestured with a nod of his head to one of the younger men and the man immediately got up to go find Red Cloud. To my surprise, Red Cloud was seated with us in less than thirty minutes.

Red Cloud didn't speak Spanish very well so Marcelino trans-lated for Jesús with a little bit of my help. While speaking, Red Cloud focused his attention on the Chief that we had brought. The first part of the discussion revolved around the reason for the peyote ceremony and Jesús passionately described being sent by the Grandfather Fire to help with the problem of the shortage of medicine for the people and the reasons behind it.

"Yes, this is a complex problem that we have been considering for many years," Red Cloud said while still staring at the Chief. "Increased

consumption throughout the years as the NAC has grown, root plowing of the land by ranchers where the medicine grows, and now the
giant fences and patrolmen for private deer hunting for lots of money.
We cannot legally bring the medicine from Mexico, nor can we legally
cultivate it."

A long period of silence fell upon the group. Then Red Cloud,
looking straight at Jesús said, "This a problem of major importance. We
have tried various avenues to come up with solutions, including conducting peyote meetings, but always there are roadblocks. Your people
have an ancient and unbroken relationship with the medicine, much
longer than our tribes; if you will speak through the Chief, I will conduct the ceremony."

"We will all speak through the Chief," Jesús replied. "Since I know
you to be an open-minded roadman and this will be no ordinary ceremony, I would like for you to be the leader, Marcelino the cedar man,
and James the fire man. The drummer, water bearer, and whoever else
you choose to join us is up to you."

"You will be seated as the sponsor?" Red Cloud asked.

"Yes."

Red Cloud looked over at me. "This will be quite an unusual event
if a white man guides the fire and a Huichol shaman is the sponsor. But
in these times of great change I will agree to loosen our rules to allow
for this. However, the ceremony will still be run in the traditional way,
or in the manner the Chief guides us. Before we begin, I will need to
speak with James and make sure he understands the intricacies of the
ceremony."

Everyone agreed and it was decided the ceremony would begin at
dusk the following night. In the meantime, all the preparations would
need to be made. Red Cloud and Marcelino would invite the rest of the
participants they thought appropriate to the task of the ceremony, and
I would come back here that night to receive my instructions from Red
Cloud. Jesús volunteered himself and me to work on getting firewood
ready and help prepare the lodge.

Just before dark, Red Cloud and Marcelino joined us back at the lodge building and we had a long meeting while sitting around the fire that Jesús and I had burning brightly. The meeting began with Red Cloud explaining to me about the lodge building.

"James, I am told you have participated in many peyote ceremonies with the Huichol that are much different than this one, but you have also participated in a Native American Church ceremony very similar to this one," Red Cloud addressed me.

"Yes, once an all-night tepee peyote ceremony with Navajo people on their reservation in Arizona."

"Good. Good. I am Arapaho from Wyoming. I, and many other roadmen from different tribes, use the tepee for our ceremonies with the peyote. A tepee and altar inside the tepee are erected and taken down for each ceremony. Here in Texas, where the medicine grows, there are many different tribes that come from all across the country to obtain the medicine. Some of us, including Marcelino, decided to make a more permanent structure so it would be easier to have our ceremonies and meetings here. But this lodge you sit in still conforms to the placement of the tepee and altar. The door is facing East to the rising sun. The crescent-moon-shaped altar on the floor is about twelve inches high and wide. It begins exactly in the South and ends exactly in the North. The sponsor, Jesús, will draw a line along the top of the moon altar signifying the path or the road we will take during the ceremony. This is why the leader of the ceremony is often called the roadman. As you can see, the sacred fire is in the Center of the altar and the center of where we all sit on the ground in a circle. In the tepee ceremony one of your jobs as fire man would be to light the fire but here it will already be lit.

"You have a very important job though because you will be required to feed the fire all night. The Chief peyote guides the ceremony but the fire is what brings us all together, helps us with our visions, keeps us warm, and gives us light. You will also use a special stick to light up the hand-rolled tobacco when we pray with the smoke throughout the night. You will be seated in front of the door opening East, on its

North side. I will be seated in the West facing the East, on the other side of the fire from you. Sitting next to me on the left will be the cedar man, Marcelino, and to my right the drummer, my son Standing Bear. The sponsor, Jesús, will sit in the North. The rest of the participants will sit as they wish in the circle but once everyone is seated no one changes position. I might allow people to go outside for a few minutes after the midnight water and smoke but then everyone takes their same seat for the rest of the night. Let us all now take our positions so we know where we will be."

As the five leaders, we took our places and Red Cloud continued, "There are many things that will happen during the ceremony: eating medicine, cedaring [the cedar man using cedar smoke for spiritually cleansing people], drumming, singing, praying, rattling, passing of water to drink, sacred food in the morning, and much more. Just follow along naturally, be attentive to the fire, let the peyote guide your thoughts and songs and prayers, be respectful of others, and all will go well. Also do not consume alcohol or any other substances. We will eat a little bit of food together with all the participants while greeting everyone before the ceremony but I suggest you don't eat much during the day. I guess we will have around twenty people in this important ceremony. Any questions?"

I had a thousand questions but decided to just take Red Cloud's advice and not try to overanalyze—just go with the flow. I felt comfortable because of the presence of Jesús, and the other men seemed relaxed and supportive of my being there.

The ceremony officially began just outside the door of the lodge with Red Cloud lighting a large, rustic tobacco cigarette rolled with a corn husk. In a booming voice, he called the Creator, spirits, and the four directions, while puffing on the smoke four times. The smoke was then passed to Jesús, Marcelino, Standing Bear, and me. Red Cloud then took just me into the lodge and we fed the fire with sticks pointing to the West toward the altar. We then went back outside and formed a line with Red Cloud in front, followed by Jesús, Marcelino, Standing Bear, me, and the rest of the participants. As we entered, we each took a colorful handwoven blanket from a large pile outside the door.

Seated on our blankets in our positions, the ceremony began with Red Cloud asking the sponsor to explain the reason for the meeting. Jesús then spoke for about ten minutes, with Marcelino translating from Spanish to English. No one interrupted Jesús but there were many low sounds of *um hum* or *aho* from the participants in agreement during his talk. During his talk everyone was given a prayer smoke. I took the special smoke stick and lit my smoke then passed the smoke stick clockwise for the others to light theirs in turn. When the smoke stick made the circle back to me, I laid it on the ground exactly in front of the East door pointing East–West.

With that done and everyone clear about the reason for the ceremony, Red Cloud brought out his ceremonial case and asked Jesús to bring out the Chief peyote. While Jesús held the Chief above the fire, Marcelino threw some dried cedar in the fire and they blessed and "cleaned" the Chief with cedar smoke. Jesús placed the Chief on the Center of the moon altar making a straight axis consisting of the East door, the fire stick, the fire, the Chief peyote and the roadman. Marcelino and Red Cloud next cleaned and blessed with cedar smoke Red Cloud's sacred items—decorated staff, eagle-feather fan, rattle, and drum.

Red Cloud brought forth a large sack of cleaned peyote buttons to be passed around the circle but also stated that Jesús had made a peyote tea from medicine I had helped collect in Wirikuta. He explained that it was Jesús's desire to share this tea in the ceremony and thereby unite the hikuri in Texas with the hikuri in Wirikuta. For the next several minutes the peyote buttons and tea were passed around the circle, each person choosing for themselves which to ingest. This was done person by person in a clockwise direction from Red Cloud, and to each person the eagle-feathered fan was passed. Marcelino put cedar on the fire so each person could use the fan to clear themselves with the smoke before ingesting the medicine, and each person also said a short prayer to the medicine before putting it into their mouth.

Everyone in the circle now had the medicine inside them and the singing began. Red Cloud began first, singing the traditional opening song four times. While Red Cloud sang, Standing Bear drummed a steady rapid beat. This beat is not meant to be music as much as it encourages an altered state of consciousness and expresses the beating heart of the Chief peyote.

For the first round of singing, Standing Bear drummed for each person as we each took a turn singing, following the clockwise order. The songs were a mix of traditional prayer songs that were sung by the more experienced people and simple songs of prayer by the others. The setting was very reverent, serious, and sober. The task of those not currently singing was not only to focus and think about their own lives but to send energy to the singer to give strength to their prayers.

As I was participating in this first part of the ceremony, I couldn't help noticing the contrast between the tepee ceremony and many of the Huichol ceremonies I had attended. Although also taken very seriously, the Huichol on many occasions dance the entire night to drums and miniature violins and guitars played by ceremonial specialists. Except during the most serious aspects of the ceremonies, the children run free and play all around, people laugh and cry at will. For the main leaders of the ceremony there are obligations to perform, but for the rest of the people there really aren't any strict rules except for appropriate conduct. In contrast the tepee-style ceremony has many rules, such as keeping seated in one spot, no leaving the tepee except for the short midnight break, and no speaking or singing out of turn, among others. It seemed to me that this type of ceremony, although very powerful, was a modern version influenced by the Indians becoming "civilized" and by attending Catholic church where there are strict rules during mass. Some of the primitive aspects of aboriginal ceremony seemed to have been lost.

After the first round of singing, the drum was passed to the person on the singer's right so each person sang and each person drummed for the person on their left. During all the next rounds we did not follow the clockwise direction. The medicine was taking effect and Red Cloud stated that when a person felt the urge to sing, they should ask someone to drum for them. If that person accepted (which they always did), they would trade seats with the person sitting to the singer's right and drum for them until they were done singing, then return to their seat. I liked this drumming-singing variation very much as it did not occur in the Navajo ceremony I had participated in previously.

For the next few hours, the singing and drumming continued and during pauses or gaps in the singing the medicine was passed around the circle for those who wanted it. The atmosphere of the ceremony shifted considerably as the spirit of the peyote medicine took control. The ceremony was still very orderly but the people had shifted consciousness and the emotions and feelings of the participants opened and heightened. The songs and prayers carried a new sort of power and urgency. An enhanced sense of intimacy and kinship grew among us as well. We were all on the same road, being guided by the Chief, the roadman, the sacred fire, and the drum. We were unified to the cosmos by the placement and structure of the lodge, and through the passing of drum, song, and prayer we spun a sacred web of intentions through space and time but also specific to this particular ceremony. I had the distinct feeling that the power of our songs and prayers was being amplified by the peyote and the setting of the ceremony so that our intentions were being broadcast from the very center of our DNA out into the multi-dimensional omniverse and realms of the spirit and the numinous.

At around midnight, Red Cloud asked Marcelino to clean the altar with cedar smoke. Red Cloud then sang four special songs and afterward asked me to bring in the bucket of water from outside and place it at the tip of the fire stick. Marcelino blessed and cleaned the water with prayers and cedar smoke. Standing Bear brought over to me a tobacco smoke and instructed me to smoke four times and then pass it clockwise. When the smoke returned to me, I was instructed to put it out and place it on the altar. Red Cloud announced that we could all drink some water, and while it was being passed around he invited anyone with "good words" to express themselves. A few people offered prayers, some a teaching story, a few a personal anecdote, but all circled around positive intentions and most had something to do with the reason for the ceremony or were directed toward the sponsor, Jesús.

When everyone was finished speaking, Red Cloud stood up and asked Jesús to sit in his spot and sing for him while he went outside to talk to the spirits. A few minutes later the sound of Red Cloud's eagle-bone whistle pierced the air outside, and shortly after he returned with a smile on his face and told the group it was okay to go out for a few minutes and stretch and relieve ourselves if necessary. But he instructed to keep chitchat to a minimum and return quickly. Before returning to his spot, Marcelino cedared him.

I was happy to be outside and see the stars and feel the breeze if only for a few moments. My back, neck, and legs were stiff and it felt great to stretch out. Jesús did not come outside. When I reentered the lodge Jesús, Marcelino, and Red Cloud were quietly talking, and when everyone was once again seated, Red Cloud announced that the Chief had requested the sponsor, Jesús, to sing.

At hearing this, I felt a slight smile come upon my face. Jesús was an experienced and gifted marakáme who could enter a trance state with the peyote and sing-chant with his assistants or other marakámes for two or three straight days. I knew Jesús would respect the ceremony and only sing an appropriate amount of time but so far all of our personal songs had been rather short in order to give everyone their time. This invitation for Jesús to sing as sponsor of the ceremony was different from the personal, individual songs and I wondered how many, if any, of the participants had ever heard a marakáme like Jesús sing the voice of the fire through the peyote. I was tingling all over in anticipation.

Before beginning to sing, Jesús brought his muvieris out from his moral and asked Marcelino to tell everyone that he would be very pleased if everyone would drink some of the peyote tea made from the hikuri of Wirikuta, especially those that had not yet had any. Red

Cloud readily agreed and the strong hikuri tea was passed around the circle, after which Jesús and the rest of us sat perfectly still and staring into the fire.

Maybe a half hour later, Jesús looked up at me with fire in his eyes. He asked me quietly if I would assist him. His request took my breath because I knew what he was asking and I didn't know if I could do it. I only knew bits and pieces of the Huichol language and the closest I had ever come to singing with a marakáme was my own personal murmurings while others sang. In the Huichol tradition it is common and sometimes even expected for the people in general to answer back the chants of the marakáme but this is the specific duty of the marakáme's assistant and other marakámes participating. Being a gringo, I had never been offered or expected to be one of the main people assisting the marakáme. Basically what happens is the marakáme chant-sings a sort of verse or two, typically fifteen seconds to a minute long, then when the marakáme pauses between verses, one or more assistants and others chant-sing back the main words or points the marakáme just sang so that he or she can hear what they just said. In the trance state while channeling the voice of the fire, the marakáme doesn't know what they are singing while they are singing it. Thus the assistants sing it back for them. Since this can go on all night or even for days, the job of the assistant is almost as grueling as the marakáme's.

My quandary wasn't duration in that moment. I just simply didn't know if Jesús would understand what I was singing back to him. He would be singing in Huichol and in the language of the marakáme. The language barrier seemed much too great.

With his typical grin, Jesús assured me I'd do just fine. "We will be singing the voice of the Grandfather Fire and the hikuri Chief will be guiding us. You know how to tune out your gringo mind and merge with the fire. Do that now with me."

Jesús began his chant in a booming voice and the first verse was short and I sang it back to him the best I could. After a few minutes and many verses, I somehow realized that it really wasn't difficult at all. With the help of the hikuri, the people around me, the setting, and Jesús's incredible voice, my inhibitions and even any thought of myself had almost completely faded away. And once again without knowing the words I somehow could fly with Jesús and understand what he was singing.

I remember flying like an eagle over the Huichol Sierra as I chanted back to Jesús what he was singing. Naming the sacred sights and calling out to them. Flying over the ocean near the coast of San Blas and then over to the East and finally to Wirikuta. There he saw the Chief. But it couldn't be. The Chief was here with us in the lodge. But it was the Chief. And she spoke through the fire to Jesús and I sang it back to him. Out from the Chief came a sort of apparition. It appeared to me as the same vision of the Virgin Mary I had seen the first day I met Jesús. I started to weep as I sang and so did Jesús. Many images then came and went as he sang and I responded. Mary transformed into an image of Takútsi Nakawé, the ancient Great-Grandmother Growth. Then she transformed into some kind of serpent goddess and next into a beautiful young ear of corn that radiated pure light.

While still in trance with the fire and singing, I somehow heard from a corner of my mind a person near to me gasp and someone else say *aho*. When Jesús stopped singing, everyone was entranced and staring either into the fire or at Jesús. Some moments later, I'm not sure how long, Red Cloud broke the trance by announcing, "Let us smoke and support the sponsor with our prayers, thoughts, and intentions."

Red Cloud handed Jesús the tobacco and corn shucks to roll a smoke and invited anyone with something to share to do so. Everyone kept quiet. Jesús called for the lighter stick and I brought it to him. After he smoked, he gave it to Red Cloud who then smoked. "For this special ceremony I'm inviting everyone to smoke now. We will pass the smoke around our circle, when the smoke comes to you, you may express anything you wish to say."

Most of the participants spoke of the visions they had seen and felt while Jesús was singing. There were visions of Kahullumary, the sacred blue deer of the Huichol; of Haramara, the sacred place of the Huichol on the ocean near San Blas; Tatei Matinieri, the sacred spring near to Wirikuta; and the peyote desert of Wirikuta itself including the mountain of the sun, Reu'unar. These were all places that except for Jesús, me, and Marcelino, none had ever physically been to. Almost everyone also spoke of the Chief revealing herself to be feminine. They told of visions of Mary and Guadalupe, Takútsi Nakawé, baby corn of many colors growing in the sunlight, and visions of a sort of cosmic womb when gazing at the Chief. By the time all were through speaking, the Chief was now being referred to as the Mother Chief.

Also included in the visions were many accounts of the baby peyotes being harvested too early in their lives. Some spoke of the Mother Chief lamenting for her children and others wept as they recounted hearing and feeling the screams of the baby peyotes as they were cut from their roots. Of all the things I had seen and experienced since in Texas, this was by far the most profound. Through the singing of Jesús and the innate power of the Mother Chief, the participants directly felt the consequences, and the pain, of the millions of baby peyotes that were and still are being harvested and not allowed to mature.

A somber mood filled the lodge as many people wiped tears from their eyes and blew their noses. Red Cloud sent another round of the peyote tea from Wirikuta around the circle and then said in a clear strong voice, "Now is the time for gifts to our sponsor and the Mother Chief that has spoken through him. In this case, for this special ceremony, it is not appropriate or necessary for physical gifts. If anyone would like to gift something physical to Jesús after the ceremony, please feel free to do so. Right now it seems more appropriate to offer Jesús and the Mother Chief gifts of intention and action. It would be good if we could extend four gifts."

The group sat silently for a while, everyone looking intently at the Grandfather Fire and at times toward the Mother Chief. The silence was broken when Pepé, a peyotero invited by Red Cloud, began to speak. He informed the group this was his first peyote ceremony even though he was employed to collect the peyote for sale and had been doing it most of his life. Pepé sobbed loudly while explaining that although he realized the peyote they now harvested was typically much smaller than years ago, he did not realize the baby peyotes had a voice and that their mothers were lamenting that their babies were ybeing taken away. Pepé promised to help in any way he could to stop the babies from being taken, but he also added that he did not know how.

A local rancher invited by Marcelino, also his first time in a peyote ceremony, spoke next. "I never would have believed what I have felt and seen tonight. It will take me a while to digest all of this. But what has become abundantly clear to me tonight is that more land needs to be opened to not only save the babies but also so that the elder peyotes can fulfill their lifecycle. To grow happily in the sunshine and rain, create children, and end their life as sacred medicine for the people. I will look into opening new avenues of discussion with ranchers in the peyote zone who are root-plowing and fencing, although like Pepé I'm not sure how just yet."

The next to speak was an old, gray-haired woman visiting from Arizona. Daisy spoke eloquently through missing teeth. "I've been coming to peyote meetings for over forty years. I've seen people being helped through alcohol and other addictions, family problems, death, rape, crime, you name it, I've seen it. The medicine helps put people on the proper road. My gift is this—the Mother Chief told me something tonight that I cannot ignore. I have seen and felt the medicine work its miracles but never has a Chief actually spoken directly to me until tonight. I am humbled and compelled. The Mother Chief told me that many others need to hear her voice through the singing of Jesús. If it is the desire of Jesús, I promise to spread the word and bring people to the voice of the Mother Chief. But like the others, I ask guidance in how to do it."

After some moments of silence Red Cloud spoke. "I will make the fourth gift. I too have been deeply touched by the Mother Chief tonight. I will not get into right now all that I have seen and felt. However, one thing for me was made clear. I have a duty to try to curb consumption of the medicine. In respect to the current circumstances, we as a church are taking too much and not only the babies but the whole race of our peyote brothers and sisters is suffering. I promise to explore ways to decrease the amount of sacred peyote needed—although I will need guidance as to how to proceed."

Although not outwardly smiling, and probably not understanding precisely what the gifts were as they were spoken in English, Jesús was beaming and he knew the ceremony had gone well.

After the closing ceremonies led by Red Cloud and his singing of the "Quitting Song," we all exited and enjoyed a meal with each other while talking about our experiences. Those who had made offerings were already talking about what they could do, and I was extremely happy to see that happening.

Daisy was true to her word and invited Jesús to come back with her to Arizona with the Mother Chief and to sing in ceremony with her people. Jesús accepted and later that day I said farewell to him.

A few months later, I got to speak with Jesús on the phone and he was still in the United States. Through the efforts of Daisy and then many other people, he had the opportunity to sponsor many tepee ceremonies with the Mother Chief and he seemed very pleased by the results. In speaking with some of the people he had come in contact with, I was told that he was now being referred to as Peyote Jesus.

 # Epilogue

This is the part of the story where I tell you that Jesús is not a single person. The teachings and stories included in this book were those I experienced with five different Huichol marakámes from the core ceremonial centers of the Huichol: Tuapurie, Xawiepa, and Keruwitia. The story is written in this way to give continuity and flow to the narrative. When reading closely you can tell the slight differences between the marakámes and their teachings and tone. As described so well by one of the marakámes, Jesucristo did not come to save us from our sins. He came to guide us to our true essence and to become more mature human beings and thus closer to god. In this way, all the Huichol marakámes in this story embody the true Jesucristo. They are all Jesus of the peyote.

One of the five marakámes in this story has passed away of old age, and his iyari lives on in the family's rirriki. At the time of this writing, and as far as I know, the other four are still alive and continue helping to keep the world in balance. One of them is still very much involved with ceremonial activity, education, conservation, and renewal of the peyote in Texas and other states. Another has been a key voice in the legislation and protection of Wirikuta. One of the marakámes in this story has been made the newest kawitéro from the ceremonial center of Keruwitia—the highest honor that can be bestowed upon a Huichol. And last but certainly not least, one the marakámes is currently involved with documenting in written form (which has never been done before by a Huichol rather than an outsider) many of the ancient myths, histories, and songs of their culture for posterity.

Although the Huichol and other Natives are in a constant struggle for religious freedom, the lessons of Jesús are to me far greater than simply the spiritual usage of peyote. The core teachings revolve around awareness and perception and becoming more mature human beings. When we are operating at a level that brings forth the awareness of our true essence, we experience life free from anxiety, boredom, apathy, or blind ambition. Self-consciousness is not simply concern for yourself but a full and joyful comprehension of *everything* included in the present moment and connection to consciousness that extends beyond ourselves. In the Huichol view, consciousness is infinite in potential and is not only inside us but all around us. My Huichol teachers, using the technique of the five points of attention, constant awareness of the five physical directions and their accompanying sacred places, and the habitual making of concrete offerings, demonstrated clearly to me that by placing all or most of our attention on our ego and personality we lose sight of true reality. We must also place our awareness outward at the same time.

It is easy to think that our religious institutions function in this capacity. But basing our actions on the written words of other people is in direct contrast to learning about and living through our true essence—through direct experience. This is why purely religious thought has not accomplished any sort of peace on Earth. Quite the contrary. The world's religions are the single greatest source of conflict and war on our planet.

I believe that it is a deep connection with nature that repeatedly reinforces the interconnection the Huichol and other Native people have with all life so that they live peaceful and harmonious lives. Unfortunately industrial society directs our behavior toward anthropocentrism. This can happen despite our conscious efforts to live more harmoniously with the world. I can personally attest to this from more than two decades of living for periods of time among the Huichol and then being sucked back into a culture based on gross national product.

In the end, I am of the opinion that above all it is honesty that makes us mature and healthy human beings, which includes being honest with ourselves and our actions. We are the only species on Earth that lies. A personal commitment to pure honesty is what makes us mature. But truth cannot be determined from a single vantage point. The Huichol realize that the greatest truths have often been held by those who stood against the norm. That is why personal experience is to be valued far above religious dogma. Each marakáme must learn for his or her own self a connection to the forces that rule the world and discover for themselves the levels of higher awareness. Nature does not lie. And in that purity we can discover our true essence when we make the effort to intentionally raise our level of awareness.

# Glossary

cantador: Spanish word for singer. Often used by the Huichol for a marakáme.

Cerro Gordo: Translates from Spanish to "fat mountain." In Huichol it is Hauxamanaka, the sacred site of the North.

Cerro Quemado: Translates from Spanish to "burnt mountain." In Huichol the burnt mountain is Reu'unar and is where the sun first rose from the Earth. It is located on one side of the peyote desert of Wirikuta.

demiurgo: Spanish word for the gnostic subordinate deity who is the creator of the material world.

fiesta: Spanish word for festival or party. The Huichol also commonly use it for major ceremonies.

gringo: Term used by Spanish-speaking people for foreigners.

Haramara: Huichol sacred site of the West on the Pacific coast.

Hauxamanaka: Huichol sacred site of the North.

hikuri: The Huichol name for peyote.

iyari: Life-force energy.

Jesucristo: Huichol name for Jesus Christ

jicarero: People who are appointed by the kawitéros to serve the spiritual temple for a five-year period.

Kahullumary: Sacred blue deer deity of the peyote desert.

kakayeri: Ancient spirit ancestors that inhabit Wirikuta. Sometimes they are known to be helpful and other times malicious, depending on the situation and the person they are encountering.

kalliway: Large round temple building of a major ceremonial center.

kawitéro: Most-respected elders who have the greatest knowledge of the tradition. They are elected by the community and entrusted with this life-long position of spiritual service.

kieri: Huichol name for the plant entheogen solandra but also sometimes datura.

marakáme: Singing shaman/healer.

milpa: Field of crops or a garden.

moral: Carrying bag made of yarn and most often woven with intricate spiritual designs and patterns.

muvieri: Ceremonial wand made of brazilwood and raptor feathers used by marakámes when chanting the voice of the Grandfather Fire, for blessing and healing.

nierika: A Huichol term with many uses; most commonly a nierika is described as a portal to altered states of consciousness and often symbolized as yarn drawings and mirrors.

nineviery: Spoken words to Grandfather Fire that include intentions, offerings, and emotions from the heart.

Pariteká: Small cave-like opening near the base of the sacred Cerro Quemado where the sun first rose.

peyote: Small spineless cactus that grows naturally only in northeastern Mexico and southern Texas. It is a psychoactive entheogen used in spiritual activities. The governments of both the United States and Mexico consider it an illegal drug that only the Huichol in Mexico and certain tribal members in the United States can possess legally for religious purposes.

Reu'unar: See Cerro Quemado.

rirriki: A sacred shrine most often built in the shape of a house.

Takútsi Nakawé: Great-Grandmother Growth deity.

takwatsi: Woven reed case where marakámes keep their sacred ceremonial items.

Tatútsi Maxakwaxi: Great-Grandfather Deer Tail deity.

Teakata: Central sacred site of the Huichol located near to Santa Catarina.

tejuino: Sacred corn beverage.

tewari: Huichol term for foreigner.

topil: Security guard or sheriff. Usually refers to a younger man serving the community for the first time.

tuki: See kalliway.

uweni: Special handmade chair used by shamans and elders.

uxa: Sacred plant found in Wirikuta whose roots are used to make yellow face paint.

vara: Special staff with colored ribbon carried by officials to signify their position.

Wirikuta: Sacred desert in northeastern Mexico where the peyote grows. It is one of the five main sacred sites of the Huichol.

Books of Related Interest

Earthwalks for Body and Spirit
Exercises to Restore Our Sacred Bond with the Earth
by James Endredy
Foreword by Victor Sanchez

Visionary Ayahuasca
A Manual for Therapeutic and Spiritual Journeys
by Jan Kounen
Foreword by Alejandro Jodorowsky

The Psychedelic Explorer's Guide
Safe, Therapeutic, and Sacred Journeys
by James Fadiman, Ph.D.

The Ayahuasca Visions of Pablo Amaringo
by Howard G. Charing, Peter Cloudsley, and Pablo Amaringo

Ayahuasca Medicine
The Shamanic World of Amazonian Sacred Plant Healing
by Alan Shoemaker

The Ayahuasca Experience
A Sourcebook on the Sacred Vine of Spirits
Edited by Ralph Metzner

Plant Spirit Shamanism
Traditional Techniques for Healing the Soul
by Ross Heaven and Howard G. Charing
Foreword by Pablo Amaringo

Speaking with Nature
Awakening to the Deep Wisdom of the Earth
by Sandra Ingerman and Llyn Roberts

INNER TRADITIONS • BEAR & COMPANY
P.O. Box 388
Rochester, VT 05767
1-800-246-8648
www.InnerTraditions.com

Or contact your local bookseller